PRAISE FOR THE ~~~~~~ ~~~ FOR COUPLES

"This genius little book will teach you how to transform your conflict into closeness. A beautiful read for anyone in a relationship they want to take higher."

—Regena Thomashauer, author of *Mama Gena's Marriage Manual* and *Pussy: A Reclamation,* as seen on *Late Night with Conan O'Brien* and *The Today Show*

"The Beauty of Conflict for Couples is a knock-your-socks-off book for anyone who has ever struggled with intimacy, vulnerability, and the longing to make a relationship work even when it seems impossible. Susan and CrisMarie are absolute geniuses at helping couples go in—to greater depth—and go out—to transformational solutions. This book is readable (I couldn't put it down!), funny, warm, practical, and powerful. If you work with couples—or if you are in a couple—or frankly if there is anyone in your life with whom you are in conflict—this will become your go-to book. It has certainly become mine!"

—Ann Weiser Cornell, author of *The Radical Acceptance of Everything* and *Focusing in Clinical Practice: The Essence of Change*

"Susan and CrisMarie make it fun and exciting to learn about the thing most of us fear most in our relationships: conflict. Their stories, tips, and frameworks will give your relationship true joy, connection, and mutual respect. Every couple needs this book!"

—Pamela Slim, author of *Body of Work* and *Escape from Cubicle Nation*

"Total game changer! Follow this simple, proven, step-by-step process to get what you want in your relationship...while creating the connection and love you crave!"

—Susan Hyatt, author of *Create Your Own Luck* and *Bare*

"Whether you're navigating a major relationship challenge—like an affair—or just bickering over 'the dishes' or 'the laundry' for the hundredth time, this book provides sound guidance on how to handle conflicts when they arise, cool down, think clearly, communicate respectfully, and find creative solutions that neither of you had been able to 'see' before."

—Alexandra Franzen, author of *You're Going to Survive*

"There are many books about relationships, but not like this one. The Beauty of Conflict for Couples is practical and thought-provoking. Using their own personal stories, and vignettes about their clients, CrisMarie and Susan illustrate their methods with real life examples. They show how it's possible to access the energy of conflict to revitalize stalled

relationships, and bring more depth in shared lives together. This book will be useful for people in new relationships to establish life-giving interactive skills; it will be appealing to those who have been in relationship for years, who are looking for more depth and range in their lives."

—Jock McKeen, co-founder of The Haven, author of *The Illuminated Heart*

"Most people hate conflict and try to avoid it, at all costs. This book proves that conflict doesn't have to be scary—it can be creative fuel for your relationship. A disagreement about chores or money (or anything else) can be an opportunity to understand each other more deeply and feel more intimate and connected than ever before."

—Sherrie Toews, licensed marriage & family therapist

"Through dynamic collaboration and courageous personal revelation, CrisMarie and Susan have co-created this guidebook for you so that you don't have to go it alone any longer. They have skillfully laid out the map that will show you the way to transform time and energy that is usually consumed in bickering, avoiding or enduring conflict, or coexisting while quietly longing for that "something" that seems to be missing into deeper intimacy and more ease and enjoyment than ever before."

—Linda Nicholls, Dip.C., PhD and senior faculty at the Haven Institute

"Whether you stay together or ultimately decide it's best to split up, the concepts and tools that CrisMarie and Susan share in this little book will help you have those tough conversations in a healthy way. You'll be able to bring yourself more fully forward, gaining the clarity you need to make the decision that fits best for both of you."

—Laura Munson, *New York Times* bestselling author, and founder of the acclaimed Haven Writing Retreats

"All couples, regardless of where they are in their relationship, need this book. The authors have created the perfect guide for anyone looking to navigate the rocky waters of conflict, and they turn disagreement into creative fuel for your relationship. Anyone reading this book will find an opportunity to understand each other more deeply and feel more intimate and connected than ever before."

—Tammy Nelson, PhD, certified sex and relationship therapist, and author of *The New Monogamy* and *Getting the Sex You Want*

PRAISE FOR CRISMARIE CAMPBELL AND SUSAN CLARKE'S WORK

"I, Danny, as a male, a football coach, and a logical thinker, found Susan and CrisMarie's style, leadership, and process to be very helpful and engaging. I, Christina, discovered I was able to move out of fear into aliveness as we were coached through a meaningful dialogue. Together, as a couple working with Susan and CrisMarie, either in couples programs or reading their book, we recognized our distancing patterns in our thirty year marriage. Now, nine years later, married for thirty-nine years, our old unhealthy patterns have broken away. Our agreement to step into our own discomfort to find enriching ways to connect continues to deepen our relationship. Thanks, Susan and CrisMarie."

—Danny and Christina Smith

"CrisMarie and Susan's willingness to share so authentically provided us with exceptional illustrations of how the tools and concepts they were introducing to us could be used to work through difficult conversations from a place of feelings, values, and committed listening. During the program, as well as on many occasions since that time, we've referred back to those incredibly effective illustrations and tools to work our way through recurring issues in our relationship to a place of mutual understanding, respect, and agreement. We're so grateful for this solid foundation from which to work in growing our relationship and understanding of one another and

look forward to our next chance to connect with and learn from CrisMarie and Susan."

—George and Elizabeth McLeod

"We have known Susan and CrisMarie for two decades. During this time, they have honed unique skills which are brought to the fore in their work with couples. Their persistence in wading into relationship dynamics, naming what appears to be happening (or not happening), and catalyzing folks to dig deep and find new ways of relating makes their approach both effective and invigorating. They are not for the faint-of-heart: your relationship WILL be impacted through the use of their tools, the benefit of their experience, and the keenness of their insights."

—Carole Ames and Bill Leutz

"CrisMarie and Susan put their relationship on display when they work with couples. In working with them, I was able to acquire new learnings in a short period of time. Their ability to deliver the material with such flow and clarity allowed me to comprehend easily and receive new tools for myself that are helpful in my own relationship."

—Sam Mak

"This couple knows coupledom! Everything they share is real...full of surprises, rawness, vulnerability and intelligence. We learned a lot in terms of how to get present, slow down, hear each other, and own our individual 'stuff.' A big takeaway was how to individually take care of ourselves when reacting, and we use it! They helped us unearth some deeply held beliefs and feelings that were keeping us distant around some issues. Their ability to laugh at and with each other was so refreshing. Their differences and how they show up in those differences gave us hope that we can do the same."

—Jennifer Hilton

"CrisMarie's and Susan's compassionate, empathetic, yet direct approach to assisting couples surpassed our expectations. As a same-sex couple, my wife and I appreciated the dynamics and comfort of working with another same-sex couple. Their ability to transcend stereotypes and incorporate inclusivity in a mixed group workshop setting was impressive."

—Tara Langley and Lyndia Penner

"We have worked with Susan and CrisMarie for many years assisting at Couples Alive. They are curious, vulnerable, authentic, engaging, and skillful presenters who practice what they teach in their own relationship. They make available a full range of emotions when sharing examples of their relational experiences as a couple with others. It is a pleasure to assist them in this valuable work that they do."

—Sue and Aubrey Murihead

"We met Susan and CrisMarie through their work leading programs at The Haven. One of those programs, Couples Alive, is a place where Susan and CrisMarie shine. They offer themselves as examples of the honesty, caring, and 'being in the moment' that are the glue in a relationship. We have learned so many great tools from them to help us navigate the tough times, value who we each are, and enjoy all that we have to offer each other. We give both the Couples Alive program and the book two thumbs up!"

—Morag Ruckman and Cheryl Redford

"After nineteen years in our relationship, we realized that at some point we had become 'comfortable.' With the stresses that come with owning our own businesses, having a young family, and caring for aging parents, etc., we found that uneventful and comfortable was acceptable and welcome—until it wasn't.

"Working with you was a complete game changer. Richard and I both agree that one of the greatest tools we took home was the Check It Out! tool. We communicate for a living. We had no idea that we were entirely ineffective! Checking it out has spared us from many misunderstandings that have historically cost us a great deal of wasted time, energy, and emotion, often leading to retraumatization.

"Thank you both for helping us to find our old 'we' in a new way that supports us to be a safe and nourishing place for each other with a newfound passion for our future. If it weren't for your warmth, wisdom, and willingness to share your own authentic and insightful teachable moments, it would not have been so effortless for us to show up in our own vulnerability to dig in and do the work.

"The two of you are a perfect balance of emotion and practicality combined with soulfulness and humor. Each of your styles spoke to Richard and I in different ways and at different times. We both felt represented in your own voices. Thank you."

—Tiffany & Richard

"Susan and CrisMarie are a dynamic team that will knock your socks off. They are real, kind, and thoughtful in their approach. My husband and I were lucky enough to participate in a Come Alive program with them as facilitators, and I really appreciate how honest and engaging they are. I have learned so much about how I handle conflict in my relationships through their book and working with them in person. Susan and CrisMarie are two of my favorite people from whom to learn more about being human."

—Challayne Kenny

"CrisMarie and Susan have been particularly helpful for me in teasing out the subtle ways that I slip into 'being reasonable' or 'procrastinating' about what's important to me in my most important relationships— both at home and at work. Their programs are delightful and excellent. Highly recommended!"

—Cathy McNally, The Haven Institute

"I was introduced to CrisMarie and Susan when they came in to work with our leadership team at Microsoft. I really value their perspective on teams, conflict, and building trust through vulnerability, curiosity, and teamwork. I have reused their materials over and over with great success. Their style is real, personal, and practical. A must-read for anyone wanting to build strong relationships."

—Kim Hardgraves, Microsoft Director, Business Operations & Compliance

THE BEAUTY OF
CONFLICT
for Couples

ALSO BY CRISMARIE CAMPBELL AND SUSAN CLARKE

The Beauty of Conflict: Harnessing Your Team's Competitive Advantage

How to Have Tough Conversations at Work

The Secret to Setting Boundaries That Stick

10 Phrases to Say to Your Honey in a Tough Conversation

THE BEAUTY OF
CONFLICT
for Couples

IGNITING PASSION, INTIMACY, AND CONNECTION IN YOUR RELATIONSHIP

CRISMARIE CAMPBELL AND SUSAN CLARKE

the tiny press

Cover Design: Joanna Price
Cover image: Jakub Gojda
Layout & Design: Jayoung Hong
Graphs, charts & other illustrations: Jack Davis, DavisCreative
(http://daviscreative.com) and Ethan Swift (https://dribbble.com/EthanSwift)

Throughout this book, we share real-life stories to help you relate to the situations
we're describing. The stories told are based on our actual experiences with clients.
Since most people don't want their identities to be revealed publicly, we've changed
people's names and certain identifying details. Every so often, we combine certain
stories with others to give you a better learning example.

For permission requests, please contact the publisher at:
Mango Publishing Group
2850 S Douglas Road, 2nd Floor
Coral Gables, FL 33134 USA
info@mango.bz

For special orders, quantity sales, course adoptions and corporate sales, please
email the publisher at sales@mango.bz. For trade and wholesale sales, please
contact Ingram Publisher Services at customer.service@ingramcontent.com or
+1.800.509.4887.

The Beauty of Conflict: Igniting Passion, Intimacy, and Connection in
Your Relationship

Library of Congress Cataloging-in-Publication number: 2019944144
ISBN: (p) 978-1-64250-098-1 (e) 978-1-64250-099-8
BISAC category code FAM013000, FAMILY & RELATIONSHIPS /
Conflict Resolution

Printed in the United States of America

TABLE OF CONTENTS

FOREWORD

I remember the moment as if it were yesterday.

My husband and I, then dating a few months, were sitting in his truck in the parking lot of a Fry's Food Market on a damp, monsoon Arizona evening.

For the first time in our whirlwind, magical courtship, we had an argument.

I felt my chest constrict as I listened to him share something I strongly disagreed with. I came back with a curt response.

His voice rose and I sensed an anger I had never felt before. His normal calm, gentle voice gave way to a sharp, pointed tone.

Panic rose in my chest. Soon my inner critic was going wild. "I knew this was too good to be true. This relationship will never work."

We drove home in silence, with tears stinging in the corners of my eyes.

About an hour later, we sat down and faced each other. I forget who broke the silence, but we started to share our feelings and dug in deep to explain the source of our differing points of view. Our rigid guard was broken, and we experienced the flood of positive emotion that comes from truly witnessing each other without judgement.

That willingness to dig into hard conversations, to explore each others' sharp edges, vulnerabilities, and core beliefs has become the strength in our marriage.

In the fifteen years that have ensued, through the delirium caused by late-night soothing of crying babies, the stress of experiencing financial calamity from an economic crash, and the daily awareness of our divergent realities (as we were raised with different social, cultural, racial, and privilege dynamics), we know that conflict is unavoidable, but compassion is a daily practice.

As you dive deep into this book, you will find many stories of people just like you and me who came to a new understanding of the beauty and power of conflict, once they knew how to navigate through it.

You will gain perspective and tools that will help you experience difficult moments with your partner, while allowing you to know each other in new and profound ways.

My wish for you is that you experience the true benefit of embracing conflict in a productive way: you and your partner will each feel deeply heard, seen, accepted for who you are, and free to share your gifts with the world. You will not harbor slowly simmering resentments that invite envy, jealousy, and bitterness to seep into the heart of your home, which are felt and observed by everyone in your household (including your pets).

When truth and liberation become the guideposts of your relationship, love flourishes.

And where love flourishes, growth is inevitable.

—Pamela Slim

Author of *Body of Work*

INTRODUCTION

Falling in love is one of life's most thrilling experiences.

The first date. The first kiss. The first time you have sex. The first time you have really, really great sex. The first vacation together. The first "I love you." The first time you get to meet their friends. The first night in the home you've decided to share. So many exhilarating firsts. And then…there's the first moment of conflict.

The first conflict might be something big, like a disagreement about whether to be monogamous or not. Or it might arise because of something relatively small, like whether to buy a blue chair or a turquoise one. You and your partner might have a fight. You might have a long, tense car ride filled with silence. Or maybe nothing dramatic happens, and yet, you feel a quiet, internal shift inside yourself—a moment when you realize, "Something about this relationship doesn't feel right."

When conflict arises in a relationship, people respond in all kinds of ways. Some people feel threatened. Some people feel sad. Some feel angry. Some feel trapped. Some feel like the situation is too uncomfortable to handle—they want to walk out of the room and end the discussion, or pretend like it never happened. Some feel terrified of conflict and assume that it spells doom for the relationship, like everything's "all over."

In our line of work, we've seen people respond to conflict in all kinds of different ways. But there's one commonality, which is that most people don't like conflict. In fact, most people loathe it, or even fear it. Most people figure, "Conflict is too painful, and it sucks. Conflict means we're doomed. That's just the way it is."

We're here to present a different idea.

In this book, we're here to ask…

What if conflict can be a beautiful thing?

What if conflict is not something to be feared, but rather, something that can unlock the next (and best) chapter of your life?

What if every moment of conflict is a chance to make your relationship even stronger?

What if conflict can lead to more trust, more happiness (both individually and together as a couple), more intimacy, more fulfillment, more aliveness…and even hotter sex?

Over the last nineteen years of our life and career, we've worked with hundreds of individual clients, romantic partners, and other kinds of partners, including business partners and teams in workplace settings. What we've seen over and over is that most people don't know what to *do* when conflict arises, which leads to a lot of unnecessary confusion, stress, and suffering. Over time, we've created processes to help people work with conflict in a new way—you can take moments of friction, tension, and disagreement and let those moments launch you (and your partner) into a happier, more passionate, vibrant life.

Imagine experiencing a moment of conflict with your partner and thinking, "How exciting! This conflict means that my partner and I are on the verge of something beautiful—a new season in our lives and more happiness for both of us. This isn't bad. This is great. This isn't a problem. It's an opportunity."

Yes, it is possible to create that type of attitude about conflict.

That's what we're excited to share with you in this book.

A LITTLE ABOUT US

This book is being written by two people: CrisMarie Campbell and Susan Clarke. We're married, and we've been romantic partners for the last twenty years and business partners for the last eighteen years. We run a company called Thrive! Inc. where we offer speaking, coaching, consulting, retreats, workshops, and other services with one goal in mind: to help people realize their potential and feel happy, healthy, and fully alive. In other words, to help people thrive!

Throughout most of this book, we'll be sharing ideas together ("We") and sometimes, we'll share individual stories too ("I"). When one of us shares an individual story, we'll give you a heads-up to let you know who's speaking (like, "This is Susan, and I remember one time about five years ago…").

WHAT QUALIFIES US TO WRITE A BOOK LIKE THIS ONE?

We share a pretty extensive resume of credentials.

Susan has a master's degree in applied behavioral science and has worked as a family therapist, relationship coach, Equus coach, life coach, and business consultant. CrisMarie started her career working as an engineer for a major aerospace company. Later, she earned an MBA, and then began working as a coach and consultant for people, teams, and companies who were feeling stuck and craving changes. (And one time, she also competed in the Olympics. But that's a whole 'nother story!)

We've co-designed and run couples workshops, helping hundreds of couples over the last ten years both in Montana and at a center called The Haven in British Columbia, Canada.

You may think we even "like" conflict since we've written a business book on conflict—*The Beauty of Conflict: Harnessing Your Team's Competitive Advantage*—and have a TEDx Talk: "Conflict—Use It, Don't Defuse It!" We'll share more about our work—and our love story—throughout this book. But for now, please know that we've got decades of experience helping people to improve all kinds of relationships and get their mojo back—whether it's sexual mojo, creative mojo, couples mojo, or even business/career mojo.

IS THIS BOOK FOR YOU?

Maybe you're thinking, "Well, I don't actually know if I'm experiencing 'conflict' in my relationship. My partner and I don't have explosive fights. It's not like that."

But conflict doesn't always look like high-volume screaming or a hysterical fight. It can appear in many forms.

Do any of these statements feel true for you?

- "I want more intimacy in our relationship. I feel like we're just roommates."

- "We used to have so much fun together. But nowadays everything is just so…blah."

- "There are certain things I want that my partner is just totally disinterested in."

- "I sometimes wonder if my partner is even attracted to me anymore."

- "I don't feel attracted to my partner anymore."

- "I'm not sure if we share the same vision of the future anymore."

- "I feel like I'm always irritating my partner just by existing, like somehow everything I do annoys them!"

- "We've got a few recurring arguments that we can't ever seem to resolve, like whether to spend the holidays at my parents' house or theirs."

- "I feel like I've forgotten who I am outside of this relationship. I don't have very many passions of my own. Everything revolves around us, our life, our home."

- "I usually just go along with whatever my partner wants because it's just easier that way. I don't want to upset them."

- "I want life to feel more exciting, more alive, better, just… different."

- "I can't be myself in my relationship. I've just accepted it."

- "There are topics that we just can't and don't talk about."

Those are the kinds of things we hear from our clients. If any of those statements ring true either for you or for your partner, then this book holds some helpful ideas for you.

Before we dive into the meat 'n' potatoes of this book, we'd like to share a few key concepts with you—like Connection and Autonomy, Attachment and Differentiation—and address a few hesitations you might already be feeling.

BEING ME IN THE FACE OF WE

Most couples want a loving, connected, close relationship. This is what we call the "WE." Yet, each person also longs to have a certain level of autonomy. This is what we call the "ME." You want to be in a relationship and enjoy time together (connection), yet you also want to be yourself and have your own passions, your own time, your own projects, and your own life (autonomy). You want both! Sometimes, this can create tension inside you and between you, which can feel uncomfortable.

The ME

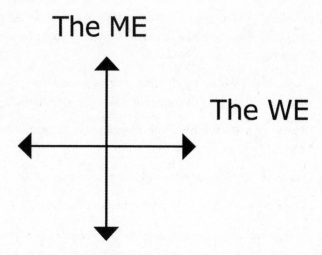

The WE

What happens is many people wind up sacrificing something they want for the sake of the relationship, the WE. This creates apathy, resentment, and emotional distance. But it doesn't have to be this way.

You can have both a strong ME and passionate WE. You can have both a sense of connection and a sense of autonomy. But this takes courage. Why? Because in order for you (and your partner) to enjoy connection and autonomy at the same time, both of you will need to try new things, take emotional risks, and experience periods of uncertainty as you both learn to navigate your lives and your relationship in a new way. All of this might feel uncomfortable at first, but there are so many benefits to relating in this way—including more intimacy, passion, and aliveness. It can seem counterintuitive, but it's true!

This type of relating isn't for everyone, however. It requires developing the capacity to ride the waves and hang in with each other in ways that most of us weren't taught to do. Most of us didn't have good models growing up. But this ability can be learned and developed. How? Well, this is something we'll discuss quite a bit throughout this book.

ATTACHMENT AND DIFFERENTIATION

When you create a relationship, you form a bond that gives you a sense of belonging. You start to know who you are in relationship to the other. Roles and patterns are developed. You know what's expected of you. Often, a status quo emerges. They do the laundry; you handle the dishes. They cook dinner; you plan the social activities. They're the creative, emotional artist, while you're the stable, grounded rock— or vice versa. As these roles develop, you relax. You feel safe. Your lives merge together. You feel attached.

Until…either slowly or suddenly, you recognize, "Wait a second. This doesn't feel totally good." It dawns on you, "Wow, this relationship feels boring, stifling, too repetitive. It's too much work—not what I want at all." You start to wake up to what's happening inside of you, the ME. "I want more out of life." "Something's missing." You feel a pressure inside to do something different—to assert your independence, to shake up your daily routine, to differentiate in some way. However, unsure of how your partner will react, you might stuff these urges back down. You prioritize the WE, and you decide trying to make that change is not for you—not in this relationship.

We had one woman tell us, "Maybe in my next life I can have a relationship where I feel alive." She was willing to sacrifice her own happiness for the sake of keeping the relationship intact. She thought she could have either connection or autonomy, but not both. Attachment, the WE, or Differentiation, the ME, but not both.

Once again, we want to reassure you that you can have both—and in fact, a thriving relationship requires both. If you stuff down the desires you're feeling, ultimately, there are consequences. You might submit to the confines of your relationship and the expectations of your partner. This can lead to apathy, or to feeling depressed, trapped, and hopeless. Or you might stuff the feelings down until one day, they explode ("I can't take this anymore!") and you rebel. As part of your rebellion, you might go outside your relationship to get your needs met—possibly leading to an affair, one that is either emotional, sexual, or both.

This is why it's so important to be honest about what you want—not stuff things down. Sure, speaking up and saying what you want threatens the status quo of the relationship. It's scary and uncomfortable. But it doesn't mean that your relationship is over. Not at all.

GOOD RELATIONSHIPS AREN'T ALWAYS SMOOTH

I, CrisMarie, thought a good relationship was one where everything was smooth. So when Susan and I got into a disagreement early in our relationship, I thought it was over and ruined and that we needed to break up.

I'd be so freaked out that we were at odds, I'd do anything to fix it. I couldn't stand the tension. I wanted to make it stop. So I'd:

- Give in

- Apologize

- Avoid the subject later on

- Keep quiet next time

While it would work in the moment, I'd wind up feeling frustrated and resentful. And then later, I'd explode, break down, and feel really stupid.

It took me a long time to realize that it's normal to feel tension in a relationship. It doesn't mean I've done something wrong, or that Susan has done anything wrong, either. And it definitely doesn't mean the relationship is over.

This is something I always emphasize to my clients. Please remember that good relationships aren't always smooth, and having a disagreement doesn't mean that you're doomed. It simply means that you and your partner are facing an opportunity—an opportunity to do some exciting reinvention and create a new season in your lives, one that's whole, vibrant, and fully alive.

LET'S TALK MATH

Each person comes into the relationship as a whole person. We'll equate that to the number one. So putting two whole people together creates a whole relationship.

1 person x 1 person = 1 whole relationship

But what happens when one person in the couple stops fully showing up—when one person starts hiding their true feelings and stuffing them down? They sacrifice the ME. Let's say they only show up halfway.

1 person x ½ person = ½ of a relationship

And then what if both people start to hold back parts of themselves, both sacrificing their ME's? Then the relationship really diminishes.

½ person x ½ person = ¼ of a relationship

The impact of not showing up in a relationship is multiplied. So the cost of you not showing up in your relationship is huge.

WHAT IS INTIMACY?

When you hear the word intimacy, several things might come to mind. You might think about physical actions like kissing or sex. You might think about eye contact. You might think about telling the truth, sharing what you really feel with someone you trust. There are many different ideas about what intimacy is. For the purposes of this book, here's how we define it:

Intimacy is the willingness to be revealed and seen by another, or said differently:

Into-me-see!

So if you're not willing to show up and be as open, honest, and real as possible, well, the relationship math speaks for itself!

TOLERATING DIFFERENCES

When I, Susan, turned 50, we celebrated by taking a bike tour to Croatia. This was a magical experience for me. I loved this vacation and was fully engaged in the whole trip.

Later, while speaking in front of a room full of clients at one of our couples programs, I was sharing how wonderful the trip was for me. Then CrisMarie shared her experience of the trip.

It was horrible. It was one of the worst times for her.

Everyone in the room was stunned that we had such different stories about the trip, and they imagined I'd be upset hearing this news.

I was shocked, since I hadn't previously heard her characterize the trip quite this way. I think because I was so taken off guard, I wasn't upset. Instead, I was curious and intrigued. I honestly wanted to hear more.

CrisMarie shared about how hard it was for her for two reasons. One, her brother had died just months earlier, so she was in a state of overall grief. Two, she had put tremendous pressure on herself to keep up with the gang on the daily bike rides. It wasn't until late in the trip she realized she could choose to go on a much shorter ride instead, or even skip the ride, stay at the hotel, and read her book by the waterside. Her experience did not take away from mine. I was honest and whole. So was she.

Sometimes, people think that "differences" are a bad thing. If you loved the trip to Croatia but your partner hated it…if you love classical music but your partner doesn't…if you love working from home but your partner wishes you wouldn't, you might think, "Oh no! We're incompatible! Our relationship is ruined!" You might try to hide your differences, fearing that if you're honest about what you like and don't like, your partner will be upset. But again, this type of hiding is always counterproductive.

I'm grateful that CrisMarie told the truth about her experience in Croatia. Imagine if she hadn't! Imagine if she had pretended she loved it! Imagine if I said, "Great, let's go back to Croatia again for my next birthday!" and she gritted her teeth, gave a fake smile, and said, "Sure! Sounds perfect!" while secretly resenting the whole thing. That wouldn't be good for either of us.

As you continue reading this book, I encourage you to embrace your differences and become even more honest about them, rather than squelching them. Honesty makes for wholeness in a relationship.

WHAT YOU'LL FIND INSIDE THIS BOOK

This isn't a marriage therapy book—and this isn't an academic book filled with research studies or historical data about divorce rates. This is a book that contains true stories about real couples—and tools that have strengthened their relationships. Of course, we've changed the names and the specifics to maintain the anonymity of the couples we've worked with.

Over the years, working with hundreds of couples of all ages, backgrounds, genders, and orientations, we have witnessed the incredible transformation that happens when couples discover that conflict is not a problem but a source of great potential—potential for intimacy, aliveness, and passion.

In this book, we'll share some tools that you can use in your everyday life. We'll offer you some questions to consider. We'll suggest some ways to be more playful and creative in your relationship. We'll walk you through a visual map of how most relationships unfold so you can see where you and your partner currently fall on that map. We'll share concepts that perhaps you've never considered before. We hope to fill you with optimism for the future.

We believe that if you're willing to bring vulnerability and curiosity into your relationship, then you and you partner can get through anything!

BUT WILL THIS WORK FOR YOU AND YOUR RELATIONSHIP?

Maybe you feel like you've already tried everything: counseling, workshops, several other books, meditation, you name it, and nothing has helped your relationship.

Even if that's the case, we feel confident that this book can still help you and your relationship, and we hope you'll give our ideas a try.

Maybe you feel discouraged because you want to improve your relationship, but your partner doesn't seem willing to get involved or "do the work," so to speak. Maybe you feel like you're all alone in this process.

In our opinion? That's okay. If one person changes in a relationship, the dynamics shift. So even if you're the only person who's willing to make some changes—for now—that's enough.

And whether you're male, female, heterosexual, homosexual, bisexual, monogamous, nonmonogamous, polyamorous, or however else you define yourself; this book can help you and your relationship. This is not a book about men being from Mars and women from Venus. It's about two people trying to relate.

Often, when we as two women step out in front of a room of heterosexual couples to kick off a couples program, some brave soul, usually a man, says, "You're two women, so how can you help us—or me? Men are different."

Sure, men and women are different, but the dynamics of relating and developing intimacy are much the same when any two people try to get to know each other, go deeper, or live and/or work collaboratively for any period of time.

Yes, there may be gender differences, but dealing with those differences is really just the same as dealing with any difference. Sometimes pulling that gender card ("Ugh, such a typical man!" or "Women just don't get it!") is just a way to avoid dealing with the deeper stuff that's coming up. The same is true if you're in a polyamorous or nonmonogamous relationship. You're still simply two people trying to relate to each other.

HERE WE GO!

Before we move along into the next section, we want to take a moment to congratulate you for being brave enough to open a book like this one.

Taking an honest look at your life—what you want, what you need to express, what's been stuffed down for too long, what would help you to feel more fully alive, how you'd like to handle tension and conflict in future—this is big, brave stuff. Many people aren't even willing

to dip their toes into this work. But you are. And your bravery will
be rewarded.

We hope the Introduction to this book has already given you some
interesting concepts to think about—concepts like the WE and the
ME, Connection and Autonomy, Attachment and Differentiation,
Intimacy, and Tolerating Differences. And now, onward and
away we go!

Onward into the most satisfying chapter of your lives. Onward into
more intimacy and passion. Onward into renewed mojo and joy.

Consider this: perhaps the very best season of your relationship isn't
behind you. Perhaps it's still in the future, still yet to come, waiting to
be created.

CHAPTER 1

Romance

Falling in love feels amazing...but did you know you're primarily having a relationship with your imagination?

You know what it feels like to fall in love. (Well, at least hopefully you do, since you're in a relationship now!) Remember back to when you first met your partner. What originally caught your interest? Was it her megawatt smile? The deep, soothing sound of his voice? Her adventurous spirit? The way he plays the guitar?

You probably remember that thrilling, euphoric phase at the beginning of a relationship—that phase when you're struck by the sight of each other. Your breath catches. Your eyes dilate. All of a sudden you get nervous and don't know what to say. You drink in every nuance of them. How his hair falls across his forehead. The deepness of his voice. The way his shirt stretches across his chest. The scent of her hair. How her red dress hugs her curves. The sparkle in her eyes.

There's usually something physical that draws us in, at least initially. However, there may also be nonphysical characteristics, like how smart and responsible he is, how he's got a fabulous job, how he comes from a good family, or that she always makes you laugh, she's so creative, and she loves dogs.

When working with clients, one question we often ask is, "What originally attracted you to your partner?"

For one couple, married 27 years, Mary, the wife, answered first. She said, "Oh, he was so smart and intelligent. We had such rich conversations. He was the type of guy who didn't care how I looked."

Ted, the husband, laughed heartily when he heard this, and responded, "What I loved about Mary is how sexy she looked in that blue sun dress!"

Interesting, right? Mary thought Ted didn't care about her appearance.
Meanwhile, Ted did care—and in fact, he loved Mary's appearance.
What does this little anecdote illustrate? Well, it illustrates that it's
very easy to make assumptions about your partner—assumptions that
might not necessarily be true. Eventually, when the truth does come
out, it can sometimes lead to tension, friction, and disappointment.
Why? Because there's a gap between what you dreamed and thought
was true about your partner (your personal Romance, the one that's
happening inside your imagination) and what's actually true.

We'll talk more about this in a moment. But first, let's talk about what
happens inside your brain and body when you're falling in love.

THE CHEMISTRY OF NEW LOVE

When you're in the early phase of a relationship—falling in love, or
newly in love—the thought or presence of your sweetheart floods your
body with endorphins. Your brain chemistry changes. You are, in a
sense, "high on drugs."

Dopamine is released, creating feelings of excitement and happiness.
Neurotransmitters like norepinephrine and phenylethylamine (PEA)
lead to focused attention, even obsessiveness—like checking your
phone 27 times a day to see if they replied to your latest message,
or "Internet stalking" their Instagram feed to see if they've posted
anything new, then analyzing every nuance of their post to determine
if it is saying anything about you. You start to zero in on the person
you desire, and at the same time, there's a feeling of euphoria.

Norepinephrine is a stimulant, so you feel unusually alert. You might
feel like you don't need much sleep. Staying up until 4 a.m. kissing on
the couch—and then heading into work at 8 a.m.? No problem! With
norepinephrine raging in your body, you've got almost superhuman
energy. Norepinephrine also enables you to notice and remember

even the smallest of details about your new partner. And then PEA is responsible for all those feelings of giddiness.

All these drugs flowing through your system—combined with your personal hopes, dreams, fantasies, and assumptions about who this person is—create that fabulous feeling of Romance.

Romance is not a bad thing. It's really fun, and it's a powerful motivator that drives us to zestfully tackle any and all hurdles involved in being together. So what if you live on separate coasts, his parents don't approve, or you're from different cultures? All that matters is that "we're together."

So yes, Romance is fantastic. At the same time, it's important to understand that your personal Romance doesn't always reflect the truth. You may have a very romantic idea about who your partner is— and what kind of life they want—but this idea may not reflect reality. Sometimes, there's a disconnect.

When I, Susan, met CrisMarie, the first thing I noticed was the sparkle in her blue eyes. She had a fabulous body and a smile that lit up the room. She was fit and athletic. I learned that she'd been a competitive rower—and she'd even competed in the Olympics.

Her keys fit my locks. She had me at "Olympian."

I assumed that with her athletic ability, she'd be a very outdoorsy person. I started picturing how much fun we'd have together camping, biking, and hiking, some of the greatest joys of my life. (But as I'll share in a moment, this assumption turned out to be very far from the truth!)

***

When I, CrisMarie, met Susan, I loved her deep brown eyes. I watched her interact with a bully as she calmly took charge of the situation, diffusing the tension in such a strong, commanding way. She seemed so powerful, grounded, and capable—like she could handle just about anything. I melted. I envisioned us working together with groups and teams and how safe I'd feel with her by my side.

We were swept away in our individual Romances—our fantasies about the other person. But again, the problem with Romance is that you're not always clearly "seeing" your partner. You're seeing a romantic movie play out in your imagination.

A RELATIONSHIP WITH AN ACTUAL PERSON—OR WITH YOUR IMAGINATION?

Sure, this person has some wonderful qualities that grab your attention. But when you're swept away in Romance, you're automatically overlooking, distorting, or generalizing anything that doesn't fit what you desire. It's as if you don't see it, or you minimize its importance.

So what if he doesn't have a job now? He's such a talented artist. Clearly, he'll be rich and famous one day soon! Who cares if she spends so much money on clothes and has tons of credit card debt? She's bubbly and captivating, she's worth it, and anyway, she always looks hot.

Again, Romance has very little to do with truth, honesty, and intimacy. Romance is all about your imagination—what you want to see, what you want to assume will be true in the future, what you want to believe—rather than what's actually true. You assume that your partner will play the part that you have cast them in. You're living in a giant fantasy of your own creation.

Imagination
Excitement
My Hopes, Dreams, Vision
Unknown
"Perfect Picture"

And most likely, so is your partner! Most people assume the Romance of their partner is the same as their own, yet these visions don't always match. Partners rarely communicate the details of their individual concepts of Romance to each other. They just assume everyone's on the same page. So, while you may have some ingredients that are similar, like getting married and having kids, the nuances and details that generate all your internal energy are unique.

ROMANCE LEADS TO CONFLICT

As you spend more and more time together, you start to learn more about each other. The truth emerges. Your partner may start to do things that conflict with the romantic story of who you thought they were, or who you wanted them to be.

He doesn't pick up his clothes. He drives too fast and yells at traffic. He listens to heavy metal, which you hate!

She's never on time. She leaves her makeup all over the place. She spends too much on clothes and never stops talking about work!

Shortly after CrisMarie and I [Susan] met, I traveled to Seattle to visit her. I was living in British Columbia, Canada, at the time. I suggested we take a tandem bike ride together. (Remember, at the time, I had a Romance brewing inside my mind—and I assumed CrisMarie was the type of person who just loves outdoorsy activities. That's what I wanted to believe!)

She agreed to do the bike ride. I was in the front, and we were biking some pretty hilly terrain. It was beautiful out. I was in heaven. "I've met the woman of my dreams!" I kept thinking, "She loves being outdoors and exercising in the fresh air—just like me!" My mind exploded with possibilities: a bike tour in Europe; a hiking trek across Canada; camping in the woods.

What I didn't know until later (and honestly, she may have shared this earlier, but Romance tends to impair our listening abilities) was that CrisMarie was not enjoying the bike ride. She was simply gritting her teeth and getting through it. She wanted to quit several times.

The longer we've been together, the more I've learned about CrisMarie. While CrisMarie is an Olympian, and while she enjoys being physically fit, her idea of "outdoorsy" is heading to a four-star resort with a view of some trees, a comfy bed and bath, and sipping wine on the deck. My romantic fantasy about who she is—and the reality of who she is—turned out to be quite different.

But does this mean we're incompatible? No. Does this mean we shouldn't be together as a couple? No. It just means we're different people. Differences don't have to be a source of pain. Differences can be a source of passion, aliveness, and excitement.

***

I, CrisMarie, experienced my own set of romantic fantasies and delusions when Susan and I first got together. Shortly after we met, I was hired by a company to do a workshop. This company had a team that was dealing with conflict, and I was excited to do the workshop and share some processes and tools. I decided to bring Susan into the project. With her background in therapy and coaching, I thought this would be a perfect match. We were going to be one of those "power couples," loving each other, working together, dazzling my client to the max!

The day of the workshop, I went to the airport to pick Susan up. I was wearing a crisp blazer and a button-down shirt with a classy handbag, looking very chic and professional. And then Susan stepped off the plane wearing a pair of jeans and a big, baggy sweater.

It was like a needle scratching across a record. She wasn't going to wear that for our meeting with the client, right?! When I asked, "Do you need to change?" she replied calmly, "No, I'm set to go." I was stunned. But I was too afraid to say anything else, so we carried on.

It was early, so we stopped to pick up some breakfast at McDonald's. Definitely not my idea of a "great breakfast," but we were pressed for time, so I figured, "Whatever. Let's just get on with it." I didn't even have time to eat because I needed to set up the room for the workshop. I was busily arranging worksheets and pens and PowerPoint slides and getting everything organized. People started to arrive. As each person stepped into the room, I would stop and greet them.

All this time, there's Susan, sitting there, eating her breakfast, ignoring the incoming people. Plus, the room smelled of McDonald's fast food! Unbelievable!

After three or four minutes of this, I walked over and glared at her, grabbed the McDonald's bag and tossed it in the trash, and said in a harsh stage whisper, "Get up and meet people!"

Susan looked at me like I had three heads. Then she calmly said, "You know your cell phone was in the bag you just threw in the trash." It was true. I was so frazzled and stressed, I'd tossed my iPhone right into the garbage can!

Oh, the irony. My workshop about managing conflict was filled with...conflict! I felt upset with Susan for not "doing things right" and not "dressing professionally." But now, looking back, I know that Susan didn't actually do anything "wrong." She was just being herself: centered, real, authentic, and casual. The only problem was that her authentic self conflicted with the romantic fantasy I'd concocted inside my head. That's why I felt so frustrated—because there was a gap between my fantasy and our reality. This type of situation is so common for couples—not just at the very beginning of a relationship, but all through the years.

A PATTERN

The experience of Romance—having dreams and fantasies, assuming your partner will behave a certain way, or wishing they'll behave a certain way—doesn't just happen once and go away. We hold tightly onto our hopes and dreams, even if the other isn't participating. We try again to persuade, encourage, and manage the other to fit our perfect picture. And again.

I, Susan, continued to bring up outdoor activities. When we moved to Montana, I convinced CrisMarie to take some long ten-mile hikes together one summer with some friends. I was encouraged because she did each one. Later, I learned she had only agreed to go because she felt pressured and because she was looking forward to some social connection—not because she actually loved hiking. We haven't taken a long hike since.

The good news is, just down the street from our home, we have state land where we take the dogs off leash every day for long walks. Both of us enjoy that.

To be honest, I still haven't given up! My current Romance is that maybe if we rent a fancy camper that's plush and comfortable (with a deluxe pillow top mattress for the bed inside), then we could go on some outdoor trips together. The jury's still out. So please root for me!

I'm grateful I still have a seed of my original Romance remaining, because my Romance is an internal spark for finding the courage to refresh, re-engage, and discover something that might be missing for me.

**

For me, CrisMarie, I had a Romance that Susan and I would work together in the corporate world...which we do! That's one romantic fantasy that did in fact turn into a reality. However, I still struggle when Susan's idea of appropriate footwear includes cowboy boots and dress jeans for a boardroom; or when I have to line someone up to do our makeup and hair when we are doing a photo shoot—and she decides to shave one side of her head just before the scheduled date! Yes, I still hold onto the hope that one day, Susan is going to care about aesthetic details and appearance as much as I do! Meanwhile, as a happy medium, I have found a few great boot stores in town, and I've persuaded Susan to invest in some "nice" jeans that are more appropriate for corporate settings. Hey, it's progress.

Nineteen years into our relationship, we're both still trying to shape and mold each other—but the difference is, today, we can do this with a spirit of playfulness and joy rather than frustration. The feeling is, "Hey, wouldn't it be fun if we could try _____?" rather than, "Why don't you ever _____?!!!"

Today, we both understand what's happening here. We understand that Romance is really a "me" thing, not an "us" thing. When I, CrisMarie, have a Romance about how I want Susan to show up in the world, it's all about my individual longings, my individual yearning for a particular kind of life, relationship, image, career, clientele, and so on.

These days, we can laugh about how our individual Romance still arises for each of us—and we can now make some choices together about how we will play along!

We want to encourage you to recognize and love your romantic roots—your early Romance—and also get curious about the romantic roots of your honey, too.

STOKING THE ROMANTIC FLAMES

One simple—and very exciting—way to reignite some juice in your relationship is to share your early hopes and dreams with your partner. What did you imagine the other person to be? Back in the earlier days of your relationship, what were your hopes for your life together?

We worked with one couple, Elsa and Peter, who'd met and married in medical school ten years earlier. Their original shared Romance was that they'd become doctors together. They'd been on the same path—but then, Elsa got pregnant. She decided to stay in medical school, and Peter decided to step off the path, become a part-time massage therapist, and raise their son.

After ten years, things between Elsa and Peter had become a bit stale. They wanted to reignite their passion. We asked them to revisit their early hopes and dreams.

As they shared, it was clear that for Peter, leaving medicine had been a choice that happened without enough dialogue. He had some regrets about it. He felt like he'd made a major sacrifice—and he'd never felt completely "okay" about it. Peter's internal conflict about his career path was, of course, spilling over into the relationship.

"Do you still want to become a doctor? Would you like to go back to medical school?" we inquired.

"No," Peter told us. He was clear on this. He didn't want to go back to medical school now. Time had passed. They had two children. But he did want some kind of change. He wanted to feel more excited about his life. He missed the way he'd felt in the early years of his relationship with Elsa—back when they were both on the same career path, back when they had a shared sense of purpose, back when the future seemed full of limitless possibilities.

Turns out, Elsa missed this feeling, too. Both Elsa and Peter liked the idea of having a shared project together, something enlivening, creative, and filled with passion.

We continued working with them, helping them to uncover what this "project" might be. Ultimately, Elsa and Peter decided to start a business together—a small-town holistic health clinic. It allows them to work together as a physician and massage therapist. They found a way to support both of their career passions while also sharing parenting responsibilities.

By exploring their early Romance, Elsa and Peter were able to remember things they'd forgotten, revive their relationship, and reinvent their whole lives. They made some pretty major career and lifestyle changes. But it's not always necessary to make such drastic changes. Many times, smaller changes can create the feeling of aliveness that you both crave: things like starting a new project together (such as running a fundraiser or planting a garden), planning a new type of vacation, training to race in a 5K event, or trying something outside your comfort zone—all of these experiences can reignite that spark.

As you reflect on your original Romance and hear your partner's Romance about you, don't be surprised if what you hear from them seems very different than who you were, or who you are. Enjoy listening to your partner's musings, imagination, and dreams. Listen through their eyes and ears.

I know now that CrisMarie isn't likely to engage in the athletic adventures I hoped for long ago. However, we have taken a couple of yoga retreats and learned to golf together, and yes, for my 50th birthday, we did take a biking vacation to Croatia—although we probably won't be doing that particular type of vacation again! When things are feeling flat for me in our relationship, I start to imagine ways to ignite the romantic spark again. More recently, as I shared earlier, I've been exploring those very fancy vans that would allow us to travel in style with our dogs to beautiful outdoor locations—and she seems willing to try it! Indeed, the Romance is still alive!

**

And I, CrisMarie, understand that Susan is probably never going to show up for a client meeting wearing a J. Crew power suit with a matching bag—and you know what? That's okay. We still get to work and collaborate together (which was always a big romantic fantasy of mine!), and in fact, our differences make us a stronger team, not a weaker one. We're able to resonate with a wider range of clients because we're not exactly alike. Some clients resonate with my energy, my ideas, and my personal stories. Others resonate with Susan's grounded, authentic presence. And when we're meeting with clients, brainstorming together about a new business project, or getting on a plane to head to a speaking engagement or workshop, I often think to myself, "There's nobody else I'd rather have by my side."

I've learned that having a Romance about your partner is fun, even euphoric—but sometimes, reality can be even sweeter than fantasy.

QUESTIONS TO EXPLORE TOGETHER

1. Separately, take some time and write down:

    - What originally attracted you to your mate? Think of physical qualities as well as other characteristics.

    - What were your original hopes and dreams of who you would be together?

    - As time has passed, have you noticed a gap between who you fantasized they would be and who they actually are?

- How do you see your original Romance still showing up in your relationship? What are your visions for you two in the future? Do they link to your original Romance?

2. Share your responses with your partner. Listen deeply. Try to cultivate a sense of humor about whatever is shared—"Oh, it's hilarious that I assumed that about you! Haha!"

3. Now, try to see if there are some areas where your individual Romances overlap.

   - Is there a Romance that both of you shared earlier or that you still share today? (For example, "Both of us always dreamed of living in Europe for one year," "Both of us like the idea of starting a business together," "Both of us dreamed about having a colorful, creative life surrounded by artists and interesting people.")

   - What's you and your partner's shared Romance? Is there some way that you could bring that Romance into your life today?

CHAPTER 2

Conflict

"Why isn't s/he doing what I want?!"

What conflict is, how it arises in relationships, and why even relatively small conflicts (laundry, dishes, etc.) can feel so upsetting.

As you spend more time around your partner, you begin to experience new facets of their personality. You know more about them. You get to see how they show up in a variety of situations—how they behave when they're healthy, when they're sick, when they're hungry, when they're tired, when they're visiting family, when they're frustrated with something at work, and so on.

As time passes, you notice things you hadn't noticed before. You begin to see that your partner's real-life behavior doesn't always match the romantic fantasy you'd created inside your mind—and sometimes, this is very annoying!

This happens in both small and big ways. Now, all of sudden, you're noticing…

- He doesn't take out the trash.

- She doesn't want to have sex nearly as often as she did when you first met.

- He never wants to go out and watches TV all the time.

- She's always telling you what you need to do around the house.

- He doesn't talk to you about how he feels when tough situations come up.

- She tends to be too emotional and overreacts to everything.

Your romance is being challenged by the reality of the person you're with. You don't like this. It creates tension inside you and between you and your partner.

This is what we call the Conflict Stage of a relationship. In this stage, you're still tightly holding onto what you think your partner should be doing and what you wish they were doing. You're searching for ways to make them behave the way you want.

So, what do you do?

You try to control your partner. You try to make them come back into alignment with your original Romance of them. This is the first step into Conflict. You're still optimistic about your chances of having your partner conform to what you want.

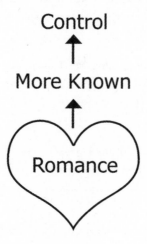

MEET DONNA AND DAVE

Dave loves to come home from the office and drop his briefcase and other work items right by the front door. He's quick to change out of his suit and grab a football to go out and play with Donna's two boys, Jack and Todd.

Donna loves that he's building a bond with her boys but hates that he leaves things everywhere.

"He just needs a little hint," she thinks. So she picks up his work things and puts them by his favorite TV chair. She neatly places his suit and clothes on his side of the bed.

Then she goes outside to enjoy seeing Dave out with the boys—feeling assured this is just a little issue and can be corrected!

CAN YOU RELATE?

If so, probably after some successful attempts but even more failures, you begin to realize this isn't working. The other person is not "getting the hint." You start to blame them for being so oblivious, so difficult.

What do you do next? You up the ante.

You complain to your friends about the situation. Your friends assure you that you're right and share similar stories of their relationship challenges. You feel heard and understood. While venting relieves the tension you feel inside, it doesn't resolve anything with your partner. Though thanks to your friends, you've gathered some new strategies to try to get your way.

BACK TO DONNA AND DAVE

Donna is loving the growing relationship that Dave is having with the boys, even though he's done nothing to shift his messy, irresponsible patterns around the house. It was mildly annoying before. But now, things have escalated for Donna, and what she's feeling is beyond annoyance—she's starting to get really angry!

She is no longer neatly laying his suit on his side of the bed. She's tossing it on the floor of his closet. When Dave asks where his clothes have gone, she gives him an icy stare and spits out, "In the closet, where they're supposed to be." On a particularly bad day, she takes that fancy new dress shirt of his and puts it in the washer! (Even though she knows it is dry clean only.) She's lashing out in frustration.

Notice the shift from gentle, loving hints (still heavily in the Romance phase) to a full-on power struggle (moving into the Conflict phase).

At this point, Donna is now at a place where she's solidly convinced Dave is just plain wrong.

CAN YOU RELATE TO THIS, TOO?

If so, at this point, maybe you resort to giving him a piece of your mind. Your tone becomes vicious. Maybe you start yelling, trying to convince your partner just how wrong they are. You give them all the data about why they should be different. Or maybe you go cold and distant, loudly but silently blaming them in your head. Either way, the impact is the same.

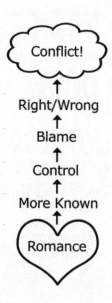

THE BREAKING POINT

Dave gets upset about the ruined shirt.

"How could you put it in the wash? You know it's dry clean only!" Dave shouts.

Suddenly, Donna blows.

"Well, if you ever picked up your own crap, you'd have put it with the dry cleaning, not on the floor where it got put in the wash. You never put anything away! You throw all your stuff by the front door when you get home, you throw your clothes on the bed—on my side—you expect me to just clean up after you, and I've been doing it for weeks! I'm sick of it! It's not my fault your stupid shirt got ruined, you don't take care of anything! I have to do everything around here!"

Uncertain about what to do next, they separate and fume.

You've probably been in a similar type of fight with your partner.

After some time passes—usually not much time, because you're both feeling so uncomfortable with the distance—you cave. You backpedal. You apologize for overreacting. You buy flowers. You try to defuse the tension (or your partner does). The next step is an attempt to make things better: the I'm-so-sorry stage.

"SO SORRY, HONEY"

Donna ruined Dave's new shirt. So she goes out and gets him a replacement. She takes all the blame for what happened. She apologizes and tells Dave how sexy he looks in that new shirt.

This results in some great make-up sex, but the issue is that nothing has been talked about honestly and nothing has actually changed. The underlying issue is still there, unresolved.

Great make-up sex is not having the crucial conversation you need to have. While it might be fantastic in the moment and allow you to swing back into the passionate Romance Stage, it's not really a solution. It's just a momentary blip—and then the cycle begins again!

THE UNCONSCIOUS ESCALATION CYCLE: ROMANCE TO CONFLICT TO ROMANCE

Many couples get into a cycle of going from romance to conflict and back to romance, over and over. When neither person is willing to have an honest conversation about "why [having a tidy house / being on time / moving back into the city / insert desire here] matters so much to me," the cycle continues, and it escalates, growing increasingly dramatic and explosive over time. This happens unconsciously, and it typically looks like this:

1. Control: You're actively trying to control your partner because it seems like it's working.

2. Blame: You begin to realize it's not working. They're not getting it. You blame them for misbehaving, or you blame yourself for doing things wrong. You up the ante.

3. Right/Wrong: You're convinced they're just plain wrong. You start to fight loudly or give up and go silent.

4. "I'm Sorry": Eventually one or both cave, say "I'm sorry," and maybe have some great sex. You go back to your romance of what's possible.

After the 'I'm Sorry' point in the cycle, you swing right back to Romance and Control. The cycle begins again.

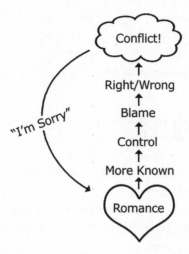

This unconscious cycle is predictable, and can be charged with lots of energy and excitement, but it's not really leading to any improvements. When you find yourself stuck in this cycle, it takes some effort—and courage—to create a real change.

FEELING "CHARGED UP" VERSUS "FULFILLED"

Many couples remain stuck in the unconscious cycle because, in a way, it's very exciting. Explosive fights lead to a surge in energy, which leads to hot make-up sex, followed by sweeping romantic gestures and apologies—flowers, chocolate, sweet promises about how things will be different. This cycle can feel intoxicating and emotionally charged.

But feeling "charged up" is not really the same as feeling "fulfilled." It's like the difference between junk food and a gourmet meal that's prepared with time and care. Sure, junk food might be somewhat tasty and it's easy and readily available, but in the long run, it's not very satisfying (or healthy).

So if you find yourself in that type of unconscious power struggle cycle, you face a critical choice. What do you really want? Do you want real intimacy? Real fulfillment? Or do you want an emotionally charged relationship that swings up and down, over and over?

RELATIONSHIP KILLERS

When a relationship remains in that unconscious cycle of control, blame, right/wrong thinking, and fighting, at some point it becomes deadening and exhausting. Either the blow-up stage escalates to the point of violence or you go to complete silence and separation.

You give up. You start seeking resolution outside of the relationship—in your career, in an affair, or by focusing solely on the kids.

These are all viable choices for resolving tension and dealing with uncertainty; and also, without any consciousness and awareness, they're relationship killers.

What is missing here is self-awareness and ownership of your part of the cycle. We are usually so busy trying to control and change our partner that we don't see our own patterns.

BACK TO DONNA

For months, Donna has been hinting and gently (and then not so gently) trying to get her point across. Yet, even with all of these hints, she hasn't said anything directly to Dave. She hasn't expressed herself honestly. She hasn't explained the deeper reasons why seeing clothes on the floor bothers her so much.

She also hasn't shown any curiosity or interest in Dave, nor has she tried to understand his side of things. In other words, she's primarily thinking about her own needs and her own romantic desires—to have a tidy house, to have a partner who loves the boys and cleans up after himself, too, to give her kids a supportive father figure. She's fully focused on herself. (This may sound harsh, but it's not meant to be.) She's not seeing the role she has played in creating this cycle. She's not claiming any responsibility. As far as she's concerned, it's 100 percent Dave's fault.

Have you been in Donna's shoes before? Or maybe you've been more like Dave in this situation? The truth is, neither person is "to blame," and ideally, both people will claim some personal ownership and responsibility for what's happening.

This requires more awareness—understanding why you typically behave the way you do, how you typically deal with conflict, and where you learned how to relate with people. Usually, the patterns of relating that we learned and that are seeded in our nervous systems go way back to our primary relationships in childhood.

TRACING PATTERNS BACK TO CHILDHOOD

Often, two people in a couple have very different perspectives, experiences, and opinions about conflict. A great deal of our personal perspective comes from what we learned growing up.

I, CrisMarie, grew up in a household with my Army colonel father. He was often angry, and at times, even violent. Every night at dinner was scary for me because I didn't know if he was going to get angry or not. When he did blow, it was sometimes dangerous. We all learned to keep quiet (or do whatever else was necessary) to calm the Colonel.

I grew up hypervigilant, always scanning the environment for signs of tension. I became very skilled at picking up the slightest clue that someone was upset and then finding a way to keep the peace. I became an expert at asking questions and letting more dominant personalities make decisions without bringing up my views, opinions, or desires.

Later in life, my ability to "read the room" and pick up on people's emotions made me a great consultant! However, in relationships, where the intent is to create intimacy, this not only backfired but resulted in a great deal of resentment and frustration.

I had never learned how to focus on what I felt, wanted, and thought, and I didn't know how to bring my needs forward in a calm, assertive way. In the unconscious escalation cycle that we've described, I was typically the one saying "I'm sorry" to defuse the tension.

***

I, Susan, grew up in a very different situation. My family was good at intellectual debate. I don't recall my parents ever really disagreeing openly or fighting, but I, as the somewhat emotional yet more physical member of the family, often heard:

"Susie, use your words, not your fists."

"Susie, use your indoor voice."

Or:

"Sticks and stones will break your bones, but words can never hurt you."

As a small child, I was the youngest, dyslexic, and often at the receiving end of my older siblings' teasing and manipulation. (They did enjoy seeing me blow!) I grew up thinking debate is great, as long as you can use big words and never get too upset or angry. The issue is that I never got particularly good at that type of debate. In adult life, I often found myself having an explosive outburst, an outburst that seemed "intense" or "extreme" to others (including CrisMarie).

Just as CrisMarie has worked to build more awareness of her tendencies and patterns, I've learned to become more aware of mine.

FROM AWARENESS COMES NEW CHOICES

When you understand where your patterns come from, then you can make new choices.

For me, Susan, this means that when I start to use my "outdoor voice" and become more heated, loud, and passionate in a discussion—and CrisMarie starts to blame or shut down, I can recognize my pattern of being a bit like the Colonel. At that point, I can make a different choice. Instead of continuing to speak loudly, I can soften my voice a bit, take a deep breath, or ask CrisMarie how she's feeling right now.

***

For me, CrisMarie, this means when I start to reflexively "manage" Susan, either by asking her a question or hinting about a different idea because I'm afraid she might get upset, I stop and become much more direct, stating my opinion. (My trigger for knowing I need to be more direct is often Susan looking confused.) I also prepare myself for her reaction, recognizing she's a separate person who has a right to her own feelings.

With awareness, we have new choices.

We often encourage couples to spend time with each other discussing what they learned about communication and conflict from their families. This starts the process of uncovering your patterns and becoming a detective into how those patterns may still be showing up.

It helps to understand how you are each wired and how that wiring can trigger your partner.

WHEN THE RELATIONSHIP FEELS FLAT

We've been talking quite a bit about fights, explosive moments, and intense discussions. But maybe that doesn't resonate with you. Maybe you can't remember the last time you fought with your partner. Maybe you've never fought about anything! Maybe you're actually bored in your relationship. It's lost its juice. You feel flat and uninspired, like you're roommates. Not all hope is lost. You can revive your relationship.

When things feel flat, it may be time to risk getting into conflict and saying something that might risk the attachment bond, the WE, but may also bring back some passion. This doesn't have to be an unconscious fight leading to an unconscious escalation cycle. You can turn it into a conscious conversation, which is what we'll be discussing in the rest of the book. We'll give you concepts, tips, and tools to help you become more aware of your blind spots, speak up more honestly, and create more connection during those difficult conversations.

WHEN THE CYCLE KEEPS REPEATING

As we've mentioned, it takes courage and honesty to break out of the unconscious escalation cycle. It might feel uncomfortable to do this work, but it can be done, and the rewards are tremendously beautiful.

Unfortunately, many couples allow the cycle to play out for months and months, even years, before finally choosing to make a real change.

What are some of the situations that commonly lead to this unconscious power struggle cycle?

For many couples, the issue of division of labor comes up often—who shops, cooks, cleans, does the laundry, plans the vacations, initiates a date night, or takes out the garbage (to name but a few).

For couples with kids, it can also include who gets the kids ready for school, who does the carpool run, who buys the kids clothes and school supplies, who misses work to pick up the sick child at school, and so on.

For couples who work together, it can be who does the detailed administration work, or who's in charge of marketing, sales, delivery, and so on.

And of course, many couples get into power struggles around money, time, energy, attention, and how these precious resources ought to be spent.

Often couples get stuck in dealing with one or several recurring issues that have been in play for a long time. During the course of this book, you'll meet some of the couples we've worked with on these types of issues.

Either the conflict gets addressed—or the cycle will keep repeating.

THE CONSCIOUS PATH: CHOOSE TO OPT OUT OR OPT IN

The rest of this book is all about choice:

Choosing to build more consciousness into your relating.

Choosing to see things differently and to speak and behave differently, too.

Choosing to create more excitement, intimacy, and fulfillment as you go through the stages of your relating.

Choosing to charge up your relationship with healthy sources of
energy (shared experiences, adventures, pursuing exciting hopes and
dreams) rather than unhealthy sources of energy (power struggles
and fights).

The choice is yours.

Even if you're the only person who's willing to make this choice right
now (if you're game to do the work but your partner is not), even
then, your relationship will still benefit. When one person chooses to
shift, the dynamic between you and your partner shifts, too. It's always
wonderful when both people want to shift at the same moment, but
even when it's just one, that's still a great start. It's not a wasted effort.
It's worth it.

NOW IT'S YOUR TURN

1. Spend some time thinking about what you learned about
   communication and conflict growing up in your family. Were
   there explosive fights in your home? Quiet, icy stares? The silent

treatment? Lively debate? Big apologies? Something else? What lessons did you absorb as a child?

2. What do you think about those lessons today? What's still working for you? What's not?

3. How do these childhood patterns show up in your relationship today?

4. Do you handle conflict differently at home versus at work?

5. Spend some time discussing your answers with your partner.

CHAPTER 3

How Do You React?

What it means to "Opt Out" of a conflict— and three Opt Out styles that may be undermining your relationship.

Here's the challenge: relationships evolve and go through stages, which is natural.

As we've shared previously, there's the Romance Stage and then the Conflict Stage. The Romance stage is oh so fun! It's giddy, euphoric, and full of exciting fantasies. The Conflict Stage is not always quite as fun, but it's full of energy and creative potential—the potential to build more passion and intimacy, to make positive changes, to create a thriving life and relationship. Whether this potential is actualized depends on how well you communicate with your partner.

Throughout the nineteen years of our relationship—and through coaching hundreds of couples—we've discovered that there are three areas that need equal attention to create healthy, congruent communication.

These three areas are:

1. **The ME.** Yourself. This means what you're thinking, feeling, and wanting in any given moment or situation.

2. **The WE.** Your beloved and the relationship between you two. This means what's going on inside of your partner, what they're thinking, feeling, and wanting, plus how you're engaging in your communication with each other.

3. **The SITUATION**. When we work with business teams, we call this The Business. The Situation is the dilemma you two are dealing with, the context, the problem you're trying to solve. The Situation might be a dilemma about taking care of the kids, buying a house, who makes dinner and who cleans up, struggling with financial issues, a disagreement about where to spend your winter vacation, or something else.

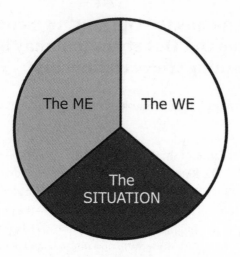

When all three of these areas—the Me, the We, and the Situation—are equally addressed, it opens the door to a productive conversation, congruent communication, and true intimacy—into-me-see—for both of you. This leads to fulfillment, aliveness, and passion.

REACTING, THE CHOICE TO OPT OUT

The problem is that in most couples, at least one (or more) of these three areas don't get addressed. Usually one of you (or both of you) will focus on one area (say, the Situation) and ignore the others (the Me and the We, for instance). Nobody does this intentionally. It just happens, usually as a way of protecting yourself from uncertainty— protecting yourself from feeling uncomfortable emotions like tension, ambiguity, shame, or anger. With our clients, we call this self-protective behavior "coping," "Opting Out," or "reacting."

Most people have a reacting style that they naturally gravitate towards—it's like your default mode. As we discussed in the last section of this book, your reacting style is rooted in your early childhood lessons around conflict, communication, and relationships.

As a kid, you watched and learned how to get what you wanted, how to conform and fit in, how to handle differences, and how to establish yourself in roles that you judged to be "right" or "best" for yourself as an adult. You've gotten so good at these patterns, you may not even be aware that anything is missing or that there may be other possibilities.

The first step in creating more intimacy, passion, and aliveness in your relationship is to understand your reacting style—how you cope when the tension and ambiguity gets too intense, how you Opt Out, and how you try to protect yourself from feeling things you don't want to feel or facing things you don't want to face.

Next, we're going to cover the three primary reacting styles—what we call Opt Out Styles—and how these styles show up in relationships. You might recognize yourself in one (or maybe several) of these styles. Try to observe this without judgment. This isn't about placing blame on anyone. It's simply about understanding what you do and when.

When you can become aware of your Opt Out Style, own it, and accept that this is how you learned to behave, you can make a different choice.

WHAT'S YOUR OPT OUT STYLE?

The following pages describe three primary Opt Out Styles that we've noticed in couples. The reason we refer to these as Opt Out Styles is because that's what's happening—you're putting up an emotional shield and Opting Out of the intimacy project.

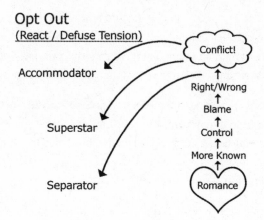

See if you recognize yourself in any of these:

OPT OUT STYLE #1: THE ACCOMMODATOR

When the tension gets too high for someone with an Accommodator style, rather than focusing on themselves—how they feel, what they think, and what they want (the ME)—this person puts their attention on their partner, the relationship (the WE), and the Situation.

Accommodators are often scanning their partner to pick up cues on how the other is feeling. Threatened by their partner's anger, they work hard to keep the peace, believing a relationship is not okay unless "we're getting along."

Accommodators have a high discomfort level with anger, disagreements, raised voices, or signs of aggressive behavior. Like me, CrisMarie, Accommodators are good at reading micro-expressions and work hard to diffuse any tension or discomfort in their partner.

What they don't recognize is that anger is natural and healthy. All humans get angry when they believe their boundaries are being crossed, when they're frustrated with a situation (or with themselves), or when they're being treated unfairly. Anger is a healthy emotion for everyone, and it can be harnessed and used in a productive way.

If you're an Accommodator, you may feel strong discomfort or even nausea in your body if you believe your partner is mad at you. What's happening is your threat of abandonment is being triggered. Your sense of safety is based on the bond in your relationship, more so than on your own need to be true to yourself and express your own emotions, thoughts, and desires.

Accommodators focus on re-establishing the equilibrium in the relationship. They'll often do whatever it takes to defuse the tension in the short term. This level of sacrifice and submission erodes their sense of self even more.

It's difficult for Accommodators to acknowledge their own anger and express it directly. In their own minds, they believe that if they did acknowledge their anger, it might threaten their attachment to their partner. Their anger comes out more in passive-aggressive ways—like forgetting an important event, making snide comments under their breath, or putting a dry clean only shirt in the washing machine. Or they may squash down their anger, and then it materializes in other unhealthy patterns—drinking too much, working all the time, obsessively exercising and dieting, and other types of self-harming behavior. Or the stuffed-down anger might arise in the form of an ulcer, chronic back pain, heart disease, adrenal burnout, or some other physical or mental illness.

Remember Donna and Dave from the last chapter? Donna had an Accommodating style. Instead of speaking up about how she didn't like where Dave was leaving his things, she tried moving them and hinting. As her frustration increased, she moved up the escalation curve and her behavior turned more passive-aggressive when she ruined his favorite shirt.

Often, when Accommodators hit their limit, they blow, just like Donna did when she yelled at Dave. Then, she moved quickly into the

I'm Sorry stage, purchasing a new shirt for Dave and trying to make peace and be agreeable.

If the Accommodator doesn't blow, over time, they can start to feel depressed, apathetic, and trapped in the relationship. They begin to believe they have no choice and become indifferent. They resort to filling a role of being a "good wife" or "good husband," thinking this should bring them happiness, which it doesn't.

Accommodator key attributes:

- Need: To keep the peace, and create harmony in relationship.

- Focus: On the other person and relationship, the We. "I just want us to get along."

- Position: Gives in, sacrifices, submits. "I'll do whatever it takes to make this fight end." "I just want my partner to be happy."

- Point of view: "Why do I need to share my opinion? It's safer if I focus on yours." "It's mostly my fault. I need to be more considerate. I'll do better. I can change."

- Verbally: Ask questions, apologize, and agree.

- Behavior: Nodding and going along.

- Blind spot: Acting out in a passive-aggressive way instead of expressing anger directly.

OPT OUT STYLE #2: THE SUPERSTAR

When faced with a buildup of tension, Superstars believe they know what's best. They get impatient and frustrated and decide it's no use trying to communicate with their partner. Instead, they'll just take action themselves, trusting that their partner will thank them in the end. This person puts their attention on their own opinion (the ME), and solving the Situation.

The Superstar style has a strong sense of their own opinion and what needs to be done. If this is you, it means that when there's tension, you believe action will relieve the pressure or "fix it." You feel an internal sense of urgency. "Ugh, enough talking and wheel-spinning. Let's just handle this already!"

You believe you have the right answer—or at least, a good enough answer—and that getting your partner on board is going to take too long. Superstars often have thoughts like, "I know what we need to do. I'll never get my partner to agree. I'll just do it myself, and they'll thank me later." And they also may have thoughts like, "My partner doesn't even know what he wants, but I do…" and "I know what we need right now. I'll just handle it."

A while ago, we were working with Meg and Tim. They'd been married 20 years. Meg had a secure nine-to-five job at the bank. She'd always been conservative with money—frugal, cautious, a true saver at heart. Tim, on the other hand, had left his secure job at the factory to start up a brewery in their small town. Three years into it, he'd had some success, but the brewery wasn't as profitable as he'd hoped it would be. Without communicating much to Meg, Tim kept putting more and more money into the brewery for upgrades, remodeling, and elaborate marketing campaigns. This latest investment was the last straw for Meg. He'd actually taken money out of their retirement savings, which made her extremely upset.

Tim was acting as a Superstar trying to make his brewery a success. He repeatedly took their joint money and pumped it back into the business. His true Superstar nature came through when he made the bold move of taking money out of their retirement savings, unbeknownst to Meg. After discovering this, Meg was crushed and did not thank him at all! In fact, she was so shattered she was ready to leave him, which is when they came to work with us.

If you're a Superstar, you feel sure of your rightness in a certain situation. That rightness can lead you to the conclusion that you know better, are better than your partner, and don't need to talk to them. You'll just manage things by yourself.

The Superstar often appears to have a healthy sense of self-esteem and confidence, which is great! However, this can sometimes veer into a mentality of one-upmanship, a level of arrogance that's actually a form of avoidance. A Superstar might think, "I'm an incredible catch, and I bring so much to the table. If my partner doesn't 'get' that, then they're a fool." "I'm awesome. If we've got issues in our relationship, that's mainly their problem. They need to get their s**t together. I'm going to just keep doing my thing, and hopefully my partner will realize how ridiculous she/he is being."

Sometimes this behavior is so unconscious that, as a Superstar, you actually believe you're doing what's best and most efficient for the couple. You really, truly believe you're doing the right thing. Your intention is to make things better. Unfortunately, what ends up happening is that you ignore, dismiss, undermine, and subtly (or dramatically) bully your partner into going along with your master plan.

Superstar key attributes:

- Need: To take action and get results.

- Focus: On yourself, the ME. "I know what's right."

- Position: To rise above, to handle things independently. "I know what's best. They'll thank me in the end."

- Point of view: "I know what needs to be done. I'm just going to go ahead and do it." "Let's just fix this already!"

- Verbal: Making definitive statements, dominant in tone and speech.

- Behavior: Taking action and ignoring concerns.

- Blind spot: Dismissing your partner's feelings, opinions, and desires as irrelevant.

OPT OUT STYLE #3: THE SEPARATOR

As a Separator, you want things to remain calm. In the midst of tension with your partner, your style is to ignore or block your own feelings (the ME) and the feelings of your partner (the WE). Instead, you become highly rational about the problem at hand (the Situation), becoming super reasonable and searching for practical solutions. Or you disengage altogether, focusing instead on an entirely different situation.

Often, it seems to you that the interpersonal dynamics are unnecessary, and thus better ignored. Underlying your behavior is a desire to distance yourself from the chaos and messiness of the situation. When you're acting as a Separator, you find the inner workings of a problem to be safer ground than the interpersonal dynamics. You appear indifferent, detached, or even dismissive.

When the tension gets too high, Separators leave—either physically, emotionally, or both. You may leave the house and go work in the garden or head out to the garage to focus on a different project. You may jump in the car and go out shopping or head to the pub.

Meet Mary and Tom, the power couple. They met at school when they were both getting their MBAs. They've been together for 22 years and have two kids, ages 11 and 13. Right after graduation, Tom got a great job working at a high-tech software company. Mary, on the other hand, bounced around to different jobs for years until she decided to become a financial planner.

Fast-forward twenty years. Tom hit a plateau in his career. After being laid off for six months, he was struggling to find a job. Mary, on the other hand, had created a thriving financial planning practice and was working over fifty hours a week. However, even during Tom's time off, Mary still does the grocery shopping, cooks the meals, and gets the kids up and ready for school. It's like she has two full-time jobs while

Tom has zero—and he's not offering to pitch in! Needless to say, she's a bit pissed.

Mary was working hard while Tom, uncomfortable about not being successful finding a job, spent his time off hiking, playing ultimate frisbee with his kids, and working on the car in the garage. Tom preferred not to hunt for a job or even to discuss it. Because Mary was in her Accommodating style, she went right along with Tom's Separator Coping Style.

As a Separator, you tend to shut down emotionally—going quiet and cold in the car, not responding to attempts at conversation from your partner, or turning on the TV and blocking out your spouse.

Two of our other clients, Kathy and Ned, were both on their second marriage. They were in their fifties and had plenty of shared interests. They even ran their own business together. They seemed to be doing well; however, when we had them discuss recurring issues, Kathy brought up that she was worried about Ned because he didn't brush his teeth regularly. This created an issue with bad breath which made him less attractive to her, but her main concern was his health. When Kathy brought it up, Ned was highly defensive.

Kathy was upset about Ned not brushing his teeth, which both made her worry for his health but also reduced her attraction to him. Before they worked with us, Kathy had avoided sex with Ned for over a year.

Every time Ned made sexual overtures, Kathy (using the Separator Coping Style) would make an excuse and roll over in bed. If Ned approached her before they went to bed, Kathy consistently turned the conversation to their business. While their business was thriving, their sexual relationship was languishing.

This desire to separate is due to the buildup of emotional tension and ambiguity around a certain situation. It's too uncomfortable. You want to focus on something completely different.

If you can't get clarity on the problem facing your couple relationship, you'll focus on something else entirely, right in the midst of the conversation. You'll check email or chat, or you'll get up and walk out. You tend to think you're being efficient or autonomous.

When you do speak up, you are often detached and calm. You prefer to focus on the practicalities of the Situation (how much to spend, where to visit, what time the babysitter is arriving, which email needs to be answered first, etc.) rather than the relationship dynamics, or you bring up a completely different topic than the conflict on the table.

Separator key attributes:

- Need: To focus on clarity, calm, and solving something else.

- Focus: On the problem or Situation at hand (or something else entirely).

- Position: To separate, detach. "I'll just go do something else."

- Point of view: "The details in the situation are not clear. Until I can understand it, I'll focus on something else." "I don't want to deal with this right now. It's not the right moment. Later."

- Verbal: Detached when speaking; can be either dismissive or completely silent.

- Behavior: Disengage to focus on something different.

- Blind spot: You avoid the problem and miss your feelings and those of your partner.

SUMMARY

Each of these Opt Out Styles is missing something crucial for congruent communication.

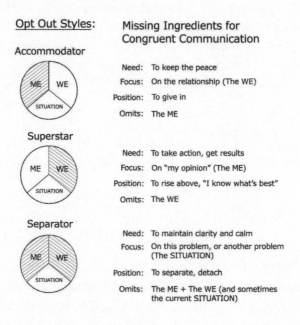

<u>Opt Out Styles</u>:

Missing Ingredients for Congruent Communication

Accommodator

Need:	To keep the peace
Focus:	On the relationship (The WE)
Position:	To give in
Omits:	The ME

Superstar

Need:	To take action, get results
Focus:	On "my opinion" (The ME)
Position:	To rise above, "I know what's best"
Omits:	The WE

Separator

Need:	To maintain clarity and calm
Focus:	On this problem, or another problem (The SITUATION)
Position:	To separate, detach
Omits:	The ME + The WE (and sometimes the current SITUATION)

When someone is coping by using one of these Opt Out Styles, they often believe they are being helpful or "handling things." However, this effort to relieve tension undermines the potential for greater intimacy. It's a stalling tactic, an avoidance technique, a way to step away from one another rather than communicating with honesty.

Your mission, if you choose to accept it, is to turn up your awareness of how you Opt Out and when. Notice how you respond when you feel tension between you and your partner. Notice what thoughts are swirling in your head. Notice what sensations you feel in your body. Notice how you behave towards your partner. Notice what you are wanting in the moment: to give in, to take charge, or to get away.

There will be times when you, your partner, or even both of you Opt Out. It might happen consciously or unconsciously. We want you to become more conscious of how you are Opting Out. Sure, you may notice your partner's style, too, but that's for them to notice, not for you to point out to them!

Either way, as soon as you realize you're Opting Out, it's time to make a new choice—the choice to Opt In, the choice to respond, the choice to communicate, the choice to build more intimacy, passion, and aliveness rather than walking away from the opportunity.

BACK TO YOU

Think about your relationship and when you get into conflict.

1. Do you recognize yourself using any of these three Opt Out Styles: the Accommodator, the Superstar, or the Separator?

2. Do you use different Opt Out Styles in different situations with your partner?

3. Which topics trigger you to Opt Out the most?

4. Do you use the same Opt Out Style at work? Or just at home?

CHAPTER 4

There's Another Way!

**Responding rather than reacting—
Opting In rather than Opting Out: How
conflict can lead to fresh and unexpected
solutions and a stronger, more
passionate relationship.**

WHAT DOES IT MEAN TO OPT IN?

In this chapter, we're talking about making a courageous choice: the choice to Opt In.

What does it mean to Opt In? It means that instead of ignoring the conflict, avoiding it, pretending it's not happening, or staying in a reactive cycle where you're temporarily coping by Opting Out (but not really resolving anything), you're choosing to explore the conflict. You're choosing to be vulnerable and honest about your feelings, the Me. You're choosing to be curious about your partner's perspective (the We) and to really listen, even if you disagree. You're choosing to stay in it and do the work on the Situation. By Opting In, you're saying, "This relationship really matters to me. I'm willing to listen, collaborate, work on creating solutions, and work on creating more aliveness and intimacy. I'm not walking away from this. I'm in!"

WHY OPT IN?

You may be wondering, "Why Opt In?" Especially if things feel really difficult and painful right now, you may wonder, "Seriously, why bother?" or "What's the point?" or "S/He won't, so why should I?"

Here's a visual metaphor that we use with our clients to show why Opting In can lead to such beautiful results:

Imagine a balloon as the container of your relationship. When there's conflict between you and your partner, it's like you're both blowing air into that balloon. All of that air builds up and creates lots of pressure against the edges of the balloon, tons of intensity, and lots of energy—which is a good thing! Energy is great! You can harness all of that energy and use it to create more passion, aliveness, and intimacy in your relationship.

You might think, "But conflict doesn't feel good! I don't like it when the balloon is filling up! It feels like it's going to pop in my face." Sure, when you and your partner have different perspectives, different priorities, or different needs, it doesn't always feel good initially. In fact, for most couples, these differences can feel threatening to your safety and security. That's because you're uncomfortable with the feelings of distance, tension, and uncertainty that conflict often brings up.

However, all those differences are a source of potential energy to be used for good and creativity. This book can help you develop the capacity to use that potential energy in the balloon. Your relationship can flex and move, rather than popping or deflating. Your relationship can stretch and grow. Your relationship will become more resilient and more buoyant. Don't you want that?

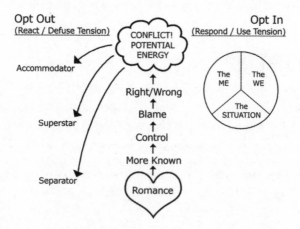

If you choose to Opt Out—by staying in that reactive coping pattern that we discussed earlier in this book—it's like you're letting all of the air out of the balloon or letting it pop: all of that potential—gone. Eventually, you and your partner get stuck in that unconscious cycle of Romance—Conflict—Opt Out—Romance, over and over. It's exhausting and not very fulfilling, and trust and goodwill diminish. Meanwhile, all of that precious air is being let out of the balloon—and all of that air/energy has to go somewhere. Perhaps you pour all of that energy into work, the house, the kids, dealing with your health issues, or possibly other people, maybe even an emotional or physical affair. Typically, this leads to a breakup, divorce, or separation—the end of the relationship.

Since you've picked up this book and you've gotten this far, we're guessing you don't want your relationship to end. You just want things to change.

Something in your relationship is not to your liking, and you want things to be different. See if you relate to any of these sentiments:

- "We have the same fight over and over again. It's exhausting."

- "I don't bother bringing it up. It's not worth the trouble."

- "I feel so alone. I have to do everything."

- "I crave emotional connection with my partner."

- "I feel like we're just roommates."

If you relate to any of these comments, we want to assure you that there's hope—and there's another way to handle conflict when it arises. You can make a different choice. You can decide to Opt In rather than Opting Out. Opting In changes everything. Even when only one person (say, you) chooses to Opt In, it still shifts the dynamic between you and your partner and opens the door to all kinds of positive changes.

Opting In isn't always easy. Often, it means tolerating a period of temporary discomfort and hanging in there for the long haul. But the rewards are so worth it. When you choose to Opt In, you have the opportunity to experience a whole new level of emotional connection, intimacy, passion, aliveness, and a feeling of "we're in this together," and you'll be able to find amazing solutions to whatever problems have been arising.

We're guessing you do want to Opt In. That's why you opened this book. That's why you're here, reading this page. You may simply be wondering, "But how?" That's what we'll share next.

CHOOSING TO OPT IN: THE TWO MAGIC INGREDIENTS

To Opt In, you need two magic ingredients:

1. Vulnerability

2. Curiosity

Let's look at each one.

VULNERABILITY

We don't know too many people who like the concept of vulnerability, except maybe Dr. Brené Brown, who's made her career researching, writing, and speaking about it. (Watch her TED talks on "The power of vulnerability" and "Listening to shame." They're amazing.) Thank goodness for Dr. Brown's work, because she's given vulnerability a space in popular culture.

Here's what we mean when we talk about vulnerability as it relates to a relationship:

Vulnerability is not about "being weak." Vulnerability is the willingness to expose oneself to danger. What type of danger? We're not talking about physical danger. We're talking about emotional danger, like the danger of being rejected by the one you love most; the danger of having your feelings hurt; the danger of hearing the painful words that you don't want to hear; the danger of feeling misunderstood or abandoned; or the danger of upsetting your partner so much that they decide to leave and you wind up alone.

Vulnerability is about taking a risk, being honest about what's happening inside you, and revealing what you're actually thinking, feeling, and wanting—even at the risk of causing upset, distance, and yes, more conflict. It's about being real even though your brain might be saying, "Yikes! Danger! Danger!" Vulnerability, ultimately, is about courage.

Vulnerability lives along a spectrum on the ME Axis. Are you going to be real or are you going to stay hidden?

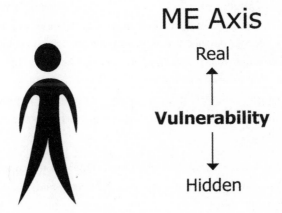

Being vulnerable often requires you to say "that one thing" you really don't want to say, which might be: "I'm scared that if I tell you what I want, you'll reject me, laugh at me, or leave me." "I am embarrassed about what I did." "I feel jealous of your success, and I'm worried you'll leave me behind."

Or in the heat of the moment, it might be: "I'm yelling because I feel really defensive right now." "I have no idea how to do this." "I feel angry, hurt, uncomfortable, or ashamed."

The act of being vulnerable is letting go of the desire to be right, to defend yourself, or to manipulate the situation to your own advantage. Instead, it's the willingness to drop your armor, reveal, and acknowledge what is happening for you. It's the willingness to share how you are feeling in this moment, what you are thinking, and what you are wanting.

NO, IT'S NOT EASY

When you and your partner are smack-dab in the middle of conflict, being vulnerable is probably the last thing you want to do. Instead, your instinct might be to protect yourself—to put on your armor and avoid putting yourself in the path of any additional pain. You may start viewing your partner as your enemy, the one who is standing between you and what you really want. You may be busily thinking about how you can convince, persuade, and outsmart your partner to do what you want. All this is, essentially, is you trying to protect yourself from experiencing discomfort or pain—which is the opposite of vulnerability.

Vulnerability can be messy. But when one partner has the courage to be vulnerable, to drop in and reveal what isn't being said, the whole couple dynamic shifts. The conversation gets real, and from there, transformation can occur.

VULNERABILITY CAN LEAD TO BREAKTHROUGH

Remember Meg and Tim from Chapter 3? Tim kept taking money from their retirement account without Meg's knowledge or permission and putting it into his brewery business. Meg and Tim attended a four-day couples workshop with us. When I, CrisMarie, went over to work with them, their money discussion kept escalating. Meg was ready to walk out of the room and get on the next plane back home. She was on the brink of Opting Out—and understandably so! She was hurt and pissed off. She didn't want to experience any more pain.

We did some coaching with Tim and encouraged him to let down his guard and speak honestly about his feelings. It was hard for him at first. But the moment he chose to be vulnerable, the dynamic shifted. He set aside his bravado, dropped into his emotions, and began to speak honestly and openly for the first time in a long while. He acknowledged that the reason he didn't tell Meg about it when he took the money from their retirement fund was because he felt like such a failure. He never intended to hurt Meg. He was just trying to make his business function, and he was ashamed that it wasn't working out.

"I made such big promises to you when I started the business," he explained to Meg, as emotion welled in his eyes. "I just couldn't bear it that I was letting you down for the third year in a row. I thought okay, I've figured it out. This is the last time I'll need to take money out of the account."

Meg was stunned. She truly didn't know that Tim had been carrying these heavy feelings of stress, anxiety, and shame. After Tim spoke from his vulnerability, Meg viewed him in a different light. He was no longer "the enemy." He was the man she loved—a man with good intentions—who wanted to be successful and provide a good life for his family, but who was struggling to make it happen.

When Meg responded, she was equally vulnerable, "Honestly, I've been so angry and hurt that I couldn't even hear you," she told Tim. Then Meg followed up with, "But Tim, don't you know we're in this together? I'm on your side." It was a breakthrough moment for this longtime couple. Because of their vulnerability, both Meg and Tim were able to realize, "You've been in pain. I've been in pain, too. But we're on this journey together, and neither of us needs to feel alone. We're a team."

VULNERABILITY REQUIRES SURRENDER

Vulnerability isn't easy. When you open up, you don't get to control how your partner responds. You have to surrender to whatever happens next, which can be terrifying—because when you share how you're really feeling, what happens next could be…anything! Who knows? Maybe your partner will respond with something you don't expect. Maybe you'll experience even more pain; or maybe a beautiful breakthrough will happen, like the one Meg and Tim experienced. Or maybe there will be more tension for a short while, but it will ultimately lead both of you towards a great solution.

Kathy and Ned (remember them from earlier in the book?) also attended our couples workshop. I [Susan] came over to help them through their hot issue of Ned neglecting to brush his teeth. After some coaching, Kathy was ready to be vulnerable. When she shared how she was worried about Ned's dental health, Ned listened. However, when Kathy went on to say, "I also need to let you know I don't want to have sex with you because your breath smells bad," Ned got defensive and attacked Kathy in return, saying, "Hey, you're not the only one who doesn't want to have sex. Look at you. You've let yourself go."

Kathy shot back, "Oh my god, that is a horrible thing to say!" She seemed angry and hurt. Susan called a time-out.

It wasn't until the second to last day of the workshop that Ned finally dropped into his own emotions and acknowledged, "I don't know what happened. I was so embarrassed when you talked about my breath—it really hurt my feelings. I guess I just felt really rejected."

Yes, it can be scary to be vulnerable and honest, but the benefits are huge. The moment you decide to be vulnerable, you shift from trying to defend against, manipulate, manage, or control your partner. You land squarely in your own shoes, finally saying what's true for you. It can be a tremendous relief when you admit out loud what's really happening.

When Kathy was vulnerable, even though Ned didn't respond the way Kathy wanted, she felt so relieved after she had shared what was really going on for her. Yes, she had to tolerate Ned being mean right back and defensive and distant for some time. However, because she had finally revealed what she had held back for months, she felt solid in her own shoes. She could even have empathy for Ned in his defensiveness.

When you are vulnerable, you have a chance to be seen and heard for who you really are, rather than as who you're pretending to be. You have a chance to take responsibility for your own experience rather than trying to get your partner to take care of you. This is amazingly emancipating.

Plus, when you are vulnerable, you gain the ability and courage to move forward proactively because you're not holding things back. All that energy you were using to protect, defend, control, or manipulate is freed up, and there's so much more energy for coming up with co-creative solutions.

Finally, vulnerability re-establishes trust and goodwill in your partnership, which then feels so much more grounding, supportive, and real. That's why vulnerability is a crucial ingredient for Opting In. The second ingredient is curiosity. But before we discuss curiosity, let's talk about…being judgmental.

WE ALL MAKE JUDGMENTS

Vulnerability is powerful and can lead to incredible breakthroughs. Yet despite the innumerable benefits of vulnerability, most people avoid it. This is partially because they don't want to come across as judgmental. Let's face it, it's pretty tough to say, "Your breath stinks" or "You're looking pretty flabby these days" or "You've been terrible with our money" without sounding like a harsh judge in a stern, frightening courtroom!

But here's the reality: You are judgmental. We all are. You make judgments all day, every day. You make judgments about what to eat for breakfast, what to wear, what type of career to pursue, which types of friendships to include in your life, which security system to install in your home, which mobile phone service to choose and which monthly plan, and so on. Judgment isn't a bad thing. In fact, your judgment is one of your greatest gifts. Your judgment or opinion is a combination of your abilities of imagination, creativity, and discernment. Being judgmental serves us. It's how we make meaning of our world and navigate our lives.

The problem isn't the fact that you make judgments, it's that you get attached to them, think you're 100 percent right, and then fight for them. We call this the right-wrong trap. When you're righteously attached to your judgments, then you're fixed in your own position. You're thinking in black-and-white terms and getting stuck in your perspective. You won't see things another way.

Yes, revealing and hearing judgment creates conflict. It's uncomfortable, painful, and awkward. But holding back your judgments and opinions not only dampens your relationship's intimacy, it also diminishes its passion and aliveness. Even if you don't speak up, the judgment and conflict is still there. It's just underground and stuck. It's air (potential energy) being let out of the balloon.

When you share your judgment directly as just what it is—only your judgment, not reality—you and your partner gain the chance to access that potential energy and use it. By sharing your outlook, your partner can provide you with a different perspective, new information, or the backstory for his or her motivation for having a differing opinion.

Remember Mary and Tom, the power couple from Chapter 3? Tom had been laid off for six months; meanwhile, Mary's financial planning practice was taking off. Mary's not only bringing home the income, but she's continuing to get groceries, cook, and clean. She's the breadwinner and the housekeeper, too. Basically, she's got two full-time jobs while Tom has none. She's getting angry, and that anger is turning into resentment because she's bottling things up. She's not speaking up. She's not sharing her judgments.

True to Mary's Accommodator style, she expressed a lot of empathy for Tom's situation. However, she also thought Tom could be picking up the slack and taking on some of the household chores. She just wasn't saying that. During a workshop, we coached Mary on how to talk about what it's been like for her during the past six months.

"I get that you can't find a job and you feel guilty about that. It even makes me feel badly sometimes that my own work is going well—because I know that must sting for you. That's probably the reason I haven't said this before—but if I'm being honest, I want you to do more around the house. I don't have time to do everything, and I'm finding myself resenting you for not taking on more of the house and kid stuff." Mary said.

Tom was quiet but did not defend himself or react. For Mary, just being able to share her judgment created a visible shift. This opened the lines of communication between Mary and Tom.

When speaking your judgments, try to use "I" statements. Own it as your view of the world, not *the* view of the world, and ask for your partner's take on it. Imagine sharing your judgments like this:

- "I don't think you're paying enough attention to the kids." (Rather than, "You never pay attention to the kids!")

- "I think you spend too much time watching TV." (Rather than, "You're obsessed with the TV!")

- "I'm uncomfortable with how much you're at the office." (Rather than, "You only care about your work, not me.")

- "I don't like how much money you're spending on the house." (Rather than, "You spend ridiculous amounts of money on home renovation projects, and you never ask me first.")

Yes, it may be uncomfortable to share a judgmental sounding opinion, but it is what you're thinking—so it's got to come out! Once you say your judgment out loud, that "charged up" feeling you might have will probably lessen. You'll probably feel some relief. What was hidden is now out on the table, and now it can be talked about!

Next, let's shift to the second magic ingredient that's required for Opting In.

CURIOSITY

Where there's conflict, there's always a choice point for those involved: do you defend your position, or do you get curious?

Being curious doesn't mean you're letting go of your judgments. Being curious means having your judgments and being open and interested in a different perspective as well. Being curious means entertaining the consideration that there's more than one reality in this world, more than one answer, and more than one way of perceiving or doing things. Being curious means you're willing to stop fighting for your "right" way and willing to be interested in other ways, too.

Curiosity lives along a spectrum on the WE axis. Are you going to be open to other ideas or be closed off and defensive?

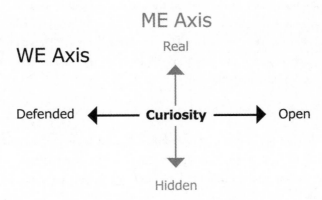

When we talk about being curious, we mean pausing, considering, and honestly reflecting on what is being presented. Even if your partner shares an idea that seems insane to you, they likely came to it with good reason. The challenge is to not assume you know what's right or best, but instead, pause and try to understand—though not necessarily agree with—how your partner came to that crazy position.

No, it's not easy. When you're passionate about something and have a strong opinion, it's difficult to pause and listen, much less reflect and consider your partner's perspective. Still, whenever we do this with each other, or when we witness another couple's curiosity, it's powerful. Amazing shifts happen. We've seen this over and over again.

Reggie and Jane had been married for 12 years, the second relationship for both of them. Jane was a brilliant and prolific cook who regularly hosted dinner parties for their friends and baked fabulous desserts. While Reggie loved Jane's cooking, he hated the complete mess the kitchen was left in when she was done. Jane was content to let the dishes sit until the next morning. Reggie, however, was used to everything being in its place. Reggie appreciated her culinary talents, albeit perhaps a bit too much; in the previous four years, his weight had increased dramatically.

When Jane, the fabulous but messy cook, and Reggie, the one who wound up cleaning up the messes, were in our couples workshop, their dialogue started as a bit of a war. Jane sounded angry and hurt. "I can't believe you're so mad at me just for making a mess! Do you know how much work it is to create those kind of gourmet meals? You don't hear our friends complaining?"

Reggie shot back, "Hey, they don't have to clean up after you!"

We called a time-out and suggested they each try to be curious about the other person. It was Jane who tried it first. She asked Reggie, "Why is it such a big deal if I wait until the next morning to do the dishes?"

Reggie responded, "I think it must come from my military training. It makes my skin crawl to leave the kitchen a mess overnight. It wasn't an option for me in the military." He paused, and with some coaching, he asked, "Why is it so important for you to wait until the next morning to do the dishes?"

"I'm usually exhausted from cooking. Plus, if we're having people over for a meal, I don't want to immediately jump up and clean. I want to spend time relaxing with you and our friends," Jane responded.

When Jane and Reggie were able to hear what was behind each other's actions, the energy charge of the grudges they had against each other lessened. They could at least understand what was driving the other person's behavior—even if they still disagreed. This little bit of space allowed them to move forward together to come up with some co-creative solutions.

And eventually, they did come up with a great solution. They had converted their garage into an apartment, and they had a tenant living there. This tenant was young, early twenties, and was always looking for ways to earn a little extra cash. They decided to hire their tenant to handle kitchen cleanup duty a few nights a month. This way, Jane could whip up her culinary masterpieces without having to clean afterward—she had some help! And Reggie could enjoy a tidy space—which allowed him to relax. They could both enjoy the dinner party, savor the delicious food, and have quality time with their guests instead of fretting about the kitchen. This felt like a win-win strategy for everyone! But Jane and Reggie weren't able to arrive at this solution until they both showed some vulnerability and curiosity. Those two magic ingredients led them to a workable solution.

We've seen this countless times with our clients. Once there's vulnerability and curiosity, that's when a breakthrough happens and new solutions materialize. There's often a "Why didn't we think of this sooner?" moment for the couple as they realize that a great solution has been possible all along. They just couldn't see it because their creativity was clouded by anger, self-righteousness, or defensiveness. Once the clouds part, the solutions appear.

A POWERFUL QUESTION: "WHY IS THIS SO IMPORTANT TO YOU?"

Curiosity opens the space to discover something new about your partner. And we know getting curious isn't easy. So when you and your honey are feeling really stuck, we suggest you stop trying to convince them of your point of view. Stop repeating your point. Stop telling them why they're wrong. Stop bringing up data to support your point of view. Stop looking at them like they are insane. Despite what you think, these tactics are not influential. This is just badgering.

Instead, slow down, become curious about your partner, and listen. One of the most powerful questions you can ask your partner to access your own curiosity is:

"Why is this so important to you?"

When you ask this question, you have the opportunity to hear what's underneath your partner's position. You have the chance to hear what's driving them. You have a window into the underlying value, reason, or incentive for their position.

When Jane asked Reggie, "Why is it such a big deal if I wait until the next morning to do the dishes?", she was essentially asking him this question. She learned a lot about him when she listened.

Other phrases that help you hear your partner from their point of view are:

- "Help me understand how you got there."

- "What is driving your passion around this?"

- "Tell me how you came to your point of view."

- "Wow! That is very different from my view. How'd you get there?"

- "I can sense that this matters to you a lot. Can you tell me why?"

As adults, we don't always need to get our way, but we do need to feel genuinely heard and considered. When you ask your honey this type of question and really listen to their response— not necessarily agreeing with it, but really listening—they no longer have to fight to be seen and heard. This opens the door to co-creative solutions, like the one Jane and Reggie found.

OUR STORY ABOUT VULNERABILITY AND CURIOSITY

When Susan and I got together, in the first couple of years we bumped into our very different views on how to manage money. (By the way, at that time, we also had very different views on how to deal with conflict, too!)

Susan had been diagnosed with a terminal disease when she was 24 years old. Her doctors said, "If you're lucky, you have six months to live." Turns out, those doctors were wrong. However, this harrowing experience shaped Susan's beliefs about the world. Her belief system goes: "Life is meant to be lived fully—right now. Embrace this moment, because this moment is all we've got. Who knows what might happen tomorrow? You could get hit by a bus! You could die in a plane crash! You could get cancer! So use this day to the fullest!"

Susan's "seize today" philosophy is actually one of the reasons I fell in love with her. I love the way she approaches each day with such gratitude and wonder. I love the way she's able to be present and appreciate each moment. However, Susan's worldview isn't exactly the same as mine, and this became very apparent when we started sharing a home, sharing a business, and sharing bank accounts.

Unlike Susan, when it comes to me, CrisMarie, I grew up believing: "Life is long, and it's important to plan for the future." I've always believed that I had to make (and save) as much money as possible. I like having a great deal of financial security. Susan? Not so much. Inevitably, this became a hot issue for us when we were trying to make spending decisions.

When the money topic came up, I would get very threatened. I thought I knew the "right" way to handle money, and I thought Susan's style was absolutely "wrong." (Can you hear my righteousness?)

However, when we argued, Susan would become quite passionate in expressing her opinion. I, as an Accommodator, would inevitably give in to her ideas. But I couldn't tolerate it completely. So I became passive-aggressive, shifting to a Superstar Opt Out style. I secretly opened a savings account and began "hiding" money.

This continued until one day, Susan asked, "What's going on with our cash flow? Where is all our money?" At first, I was frozen. She persisted. I finally admitted, "I was terrified of spending all our money. So I opened a secret savings account."

Susan was surprised. "Are you kidding me? Why would you do that without talking to me? What did you think would happen if I knew?"

"I was worried you'd talk me out of saving, and we'd spend all our money."

Susan was quiet for a minute, pausing to take a deep breath. "Wow. Okay. Well—honestly, I feel hurt that you didn't trust me, and you know I don't like secrets. But you're not wrong, we probably do need to save more, and I'm willing to try. So how can we do this differently?"

Together, we decided to have regular money meetings where we could discuss things openly and make decisions together. Yes, I continued to put money in the "secret" account, except it wasn't a secret anymore because both of us knew about it. Plus, when spending decisions came up, Susan took the time to listen to my perspective—and I took the responsibility for being honest—to make sure I wasn't just giving in and being overly accommodating.

Now in our relationship, I feel like a full-sized person who is entitled to my point of view. Sure, every once in a while, I still go to my Accommodating Opt Out style and give in. This habit is hard to break! However, I've gotten better at catching this more quickly when it happens and nipping it in the bud, instead of continuing in that pattern.

I've also developed more trust in our relationship. I know that our relationship can withstand some big differences—and thrive—if we both hang in there with vulnerability and curiosity. Believe me, we've had plenty of conflict over the last 20 years. Knowing we can weather the conflict, no matter what arises, is pretty incredible. That, my friends, is an amazing feeling.

THE COMPASS

We've created a tool you can use to measure how you're doing with those two magic ingredients. It's called the Vulnerability-Curiosity

Compass, or simply, the Compass. It's pretty simple to use this Compass. At any point during a conflict with your honey, you can pause and check in with yourself, asking:

- How vulnerable am I being?

- How curious am I being?

Take a moment to breathe in, breathe out, and consider where you're at. Maybe you're being pretty vulnerable and saying what you honestly think and feel—that's great! But maybe you're not being particularly curious about your partner's perspective—okay, good, you've noticed that, and now you can make a different choice.

When you choose to be vulnerable and curious, it creates a shift in your relationship. You become relational, an Influencer, which is someone who can harness all of that energy and use it to create transformation—to influence positive change. We believe this is the most effective approach for relating to the person you love most.

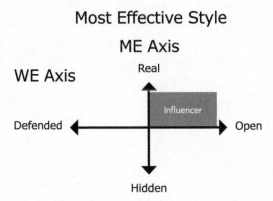

Sometimes it's helpful to have a visual aid. Take a look at the following chart. Do you feel like you're currently down in the Opt Out section of the chart, acting like a Superstar, Separator, or Accommodator? How could you shift into the Influencer part of the chart? (Hint: As always, it comes down to choosing vulnerability and curiosity.)

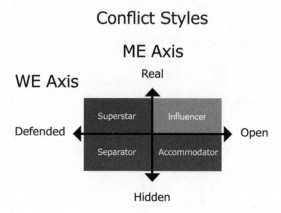

THE IMPORTANCE OF GOODWILL

The day-to-day business of life, family, and career can be a lot to manage. All of those daily responsibilities pile up and can deaden the passion and romance you once felt with your partner. Add to that the compromises you've made, not to mention all of those unaddressed "little" things that come up and go by without attention, and suddenly the relationship feels flat, or else so emotionally charged there's not much goodwill left. Especially when you and your honey are in the thick of things: fighting, going silent, and/or feeling like "this just isn't going to work," it's important to build back some feelings of goodwill.

Goodwill is defined as: "friendly, helpful, or cooperative feelings or attitudes."

You probably have natural ways of connecting that bring back these feel-good emotions. These might include doing things together that you both enjoy: watching a movie, going to the dog park with your pups, taking a walk in the woods, making a meal together, seeing friends with whom you both love spending time, or taking a day trip to the beach.

We know one couple who give each other foot massages. Another does back scratches. A third couple makes it a habit to read out loud to each other in the evenings. These little rituals can rebuild a lot of goodwill.

Susan and I take about five minutes before we get out of bed in the morning to just cuddle together. Then at some point during the day or evening, we'll put on a song and dance together in the kitchen. When we're in the middle of something and can't find a way to connect, we'll take the dogs for a walk in the woods. If we're really having a hard time connecting, we'll sit back-to-back and listen to a piece of music.

When life feels very busy, or when you're arguing intensely, it's crucial to find time to do those feel-good things together. Taking even just five or ten minutes to create some goodwill makes such a difference. It helps you remember that you love this person very much—even though right now, you may not be liking them very much.

GLANCING AHEAD

So far, in this book, we've talked about what conflict is, why it arises, and how—with the right approach—it can be harnessed and used as fuel for positive changes.

We've talked about what it means to Opt Out and what it means to Opt In. And we've shared the two magic ingredients that you need in order to Opt In: vulnerability and curiosity.

We've shared a simple tool that you can use to check in with yourself, which we called the Vulnerability-Curiosity Compass. We also shared a powerful question to use when you're stuck in a power struggle: Why is this so important to you?

In the next section of this book, we'll talk about the three different aspects of conflict—the ME, the WE, and the Situation, which all need to be addressed if you're going to have healthy communication. We present them in that order: the ME, the WE, and the Situation. Often couples want to jump to the Situation. We encourage you to make sure you pay attention and address both the Me and the We with just as much attention as you address the Situation.

We'll give you more concepts, tools, and tips to help you and your honey turn conflict into intimacy, passion, and co-creativity.

BACK TO YOU

Think about the types of disagreements you get into with your honey.

1. What are the recurring hot topics between you and your partner? (It might be a recurring argument about money, chores, parenting, sex, how you spend your free time, or something else.)

2. Think about one of these hot topic issues. Using the Compass, ask yourself:

   - "How vulnerable am I being?"

   - "How curious am I being?"

3. If you're not being vulnerable, take some time to ask yourself, "What am I worried will happen if I am honest and vulnerable?"

4. If you're not being curious, try asking your partner, "Why is this so important to you?" Then, just listen and take in their response. It's okay if you don't agree. Just listen and don't argue back.

5. What are some of the activities that build a feeling of goodwill between you and your partner? Try doing at least one this week. It's so important to keep that feeling of goodwill alive, even when you're in the midst of a conflict. It's like emotional glue that will hold you together and help you find the will to hang in there. Try to keep the goodwill flowing as best you can.

CHAPTER 5

The ME

How to take good care of yourself, stay true to yourself, and not "lose yourself" when you're in the midst of a challenging conflict.

THE ME

If you've ever flown on an airplane, you've probably heard the flight attendant give the preflight instructions, saying, "Put your own oxygen mask on first before helping someone else."

Well, the same is true in relating with your honey, especially when you want to create more intimacy, passion, and aliveness in your relationship.

Earlier in this book, we talked about how healthy communication requires that you pay attention to three areas: the ME, the WE, and the Situation. It all starts with the ME. That means you.

It's crucial to remember that no matter what's happening, you're always in charge of yourself. You have choices. For instance, if your partner blurts out something that feels hurtful or shocking, you can choose to storm out of the room. You can choose to hurl a cup of coffee against the wall. Or you can choose to pause, take a breath, and decide, "How do I want to behave in this moment? What's my choice? Do I want to be vulnerable and curious? Do I want to take a few moments to digest what's been said and then respond? Or will I choose to react hastily and do something I might immediately regret?"

Even when things feel out of control, it's very empowering to remind yourself, "I get to choose what I do next."

Of course, it's not easy to make a grounded, thoughtful choice when you're dealing with intense stress. But it is possible. For starters, it can

be very helpful to understand what's happening in your brain and
body—on a physiological level—when you experience stress.

THE STRESS OF CONFLICT

Experiencing conflict—even just a mild disagreement with your
partner—can feel very stressful. There's no doubt about that.

Different people experience stress in different ways. You might feel
intense fear, or even terror. You might notice your mind racing with
all kinds of thoughts, like:

- "I hate how s/he's making me wrong."

- "I'm going to have to do it her way or s/he'll leave."

- "It's always my fault!"

- "It's always their fault!"

- "Why do I always have to do something I don't want to?!"

- "We're never going to come to a resolution. This is hopeless."

When you're experiencing stress, you may also notice some physical
shifts happening inside your body. Your breathing becomes short,
shallow, and more rapid; and you may notice that you're tensing
up and holding your breath. You might begin to sweat. Your blood
pressure goes up. Your appetite disappears. Your vision narrows,
because your brain is trying to home in and focus on the potential
threat. You stop thinking as clearly. You can't find the right
words to say.

All of these physical shifts happen because your body is caught in
a fight, flight, or freeze response. The most primitive part of your
brain—the part that's concerned with basic survival—has been
activated. Basically, your brain is going, "Yikes, something stressful

and potentially threatening is happening. We might not be safe. Red alert! Run to safety!"

So, your brain is screaming "Danger! Be careful!" while your body is tightening up and your heart is pounding, and as all of this is happening, you're trying to think rationally and have a conversation with your honey. It's like you're trying to deliver an important presentation while crazed vultures and buzzards are swooping all around your head, creating absolute chaos! Whoa! That's not an easy situation.

So, what can you do to feel calmer and regain some control over your body? That's what we'll discuss next.

THE STRESS CURVE

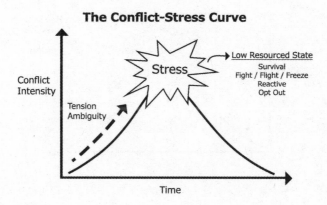

SHIFT FROM REACTING TO RESPONDING

When you're in the midst of a stressful situation or conversation, your first instinct might be to react. Reacting could mean walking straight out of the room without saying anything at all, or alternatively, blurting something out hastily without thinking it through, punching the wall, tossing a glass of water in your partner's face, shouting, name-calling, or screaming obscenities. Reacting is often unproductive and can be seriously harmful. But you don't have to stay in that reactive place. You can make a different choice—and shift from reacting to responding.

How can you make this shift? First, notice and interrupt what's happening inside of your body—and then take some steps to settle down your nervous system so you can think rationally once again.

We'd like to share three ways to settle yourself so that you can respond rather than react. All of these tools are free. And all of these tools are things you probably already know about but might be not be using when you need them most.

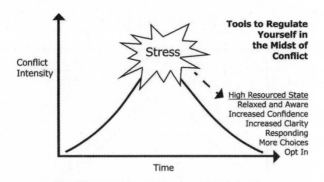

TOOLS FOR SETTLING YOURSELF

1. **Deep Breathing**

   It sounds so simple, but it really works.

When you're stressed, your breath is usually short, quick, and high in your chest. The key is to shift your breathing to being longer, slower, and lower in your belly.

To do this, we suggest you put your hand on the lower part of your belly. Breathe in to the count of four, hold your breath for a count of four, and then exhale to a count of four. Do that for five to ten rounds of breath and see what you notice.

Try repeating this for one to two minutes. If you're thinking, "I don't have time for that!" remember, it's not two hours, it's just two minutes. It's a relatively small amount of time, but the impact on your body and nervous system is huge.

2. **Feel Your Feet and Your Seat**

Again, it sounds so deceptively simple, but it works.

When you're stressed, your brain begins scanning for danger everywhere, causing you to feel panicky. But with this quick exercise, you can re-establish your sense of safety.

Bring your attention down to your feet, wiggle your toes, and swipe your feet back and forth on the floor. Then settle your feet into stillness. Imagine you have roots coming out of the soles of your feet, going down through the building deep into the earth. Imagine you can feel your feet getting heavier.

If you're sitting down, also bring your awareness down to your bum. Feel the weight of it being supported by the chair. Feel your entire body growing heavier, softer, and sinking downward. Feel the chair (or the ground, if you're sitting on the floor) cradling you.

This helps you to feel calmer, steadier, and more supported, instead of frenzied.

3. **Connect to the Space**

Notice the environment you're in.

After a moment, turn your head and look around the room you're in. Stop at an object in the space. Pause and take it in. Notice its color, its shape, and how far away it is from you.

After a moment turn your head and look around the room again and find another object. Pause and take it in: its shape, its color, and how the light hits it.

What you're doing is calming your mind and bringing yourself back to the present moment. You're inviting your mind to stop obsessing about the past and stop worrying about the future, and instead, return to the present. This room. This space. This environment. Right here and now.

The next time you're experiencing stress and you feel yourself creeping up the Stress Curve, try using one, two, or all three of the tools we just shared.

You might wonder, "But how am I supposed to settle myself down when we're right in the middle of a disagreement? It doesn't seem realistic. If my partner is talking to me, what am I supposed to do? Am I supposed to ignore them, close my eyes, and spend two minutes 'feeling my feet'? I will look like a wacko!"

If you're right in the middle of a disagreement and you feel your stress levels spiking upwards, request a brief time-out. For instance, try saying:

"Whoa. Okay, I've been caught off guard by what you just said, and I'm stressing out. I'm shaking and I feel like my heart is going to pop out of my chest. I need a minute. I'd like to settle down before we continue this conversation. How about this—let's meet back here in five minutes, after I've had some time to breathe."

Then step outside, or step into another room, and use the three tools we just shared. Once you've settled down your nervous system a bit, you'll be much better equipped to continue the conversation, find creative solutions, and perhaps, set some healthy new boundaries.

In this next section (yes, you guessed it) we're going to talk about…
boundaries. We'll discuss what a boundary is and what a boundary
isn't. We'll show you how to uncover what's driving you to set
a boundary. We'll walk you through how to create a boundary
statement, and finally, we'll go over what you can do to make your
boundary stick.

CREATING YOUR BOUNDARIES

Perhaps you've heard people say, "You need to set firm boundaries,"
or "You need to make sure he's respecting your boundaries," or "Ugh,
it seems like she never honors your boundaries!" But there's a lot of
confusion in our society about what a boundary is and isn't.

Here's how we define what a boundary is:

A boundary is not a plea, demand, or rule that your partner must
follow…or else.

A boundary is a decision that you make about how you're going to
lead your own life.

Essentially, setting a healthy boundary is about you making some
changes, not your partner. This might sound confusing, especially
because you might be thinking, "But wait a sec, I want my partner to
behave differently—they're the one who needs to change, not me!"

However, this attitude is a trap. If you're saying things like "She's the
one who needs to behave differently" or "He needs to respect my
wishes," what you're doing is you're placing your happiness into your
partner's hands. Basically, you're saying, "I'm powerless here. He's got
to do [fill in the blank], otherwise I won't be happy." Do you see how
this attitude places you at a disadvantage? It's much more empowering
to take matters back into your own hands. That's what setting a
healthy boundary means. It's about you doing something for you.

This is why setting a boundary (or "creating a boundary statement")
is ultimately a process of self-responsibility and self-definition. It's all
about learning how you can take care of your own needs, rather than
demanding that your partner take care of things.

Let's look closer at what a boundary is and what it isn't—and then
we'll share some real-life examples to illustrate what creating healthy
boundaries looks like.

A Boundary[1] :

IS about	IS NOT about
self-definition	self defense
using current information	predicting with past information
making choices	obligation and rules
curiosity and flexibility	being rigid and never changing
being body aware	exclusively thought based
contact and dialogue	monologues, threats and demands
you saying this is me	you saying this is what you have to do

---

1   Joann S. Peterson, *Anger, Boundaries, and Safety* (Gabriola Island, B.C. 2001), page
     45 - 50

We can't emphasize this enough: Setting a healthy boundary is all about changing your own life rather than demanding that your partner change.

DO YOU NEED TO SET A BOUNDARY? CHECK IN WITH YOUR BODY

Your body is always sending signals to you. A growling stomach means, "Time for some food." When the hairs on the back of your neck start prickling, that means, "Stay alert, there might be something threatening around here." Tight neck muscles might mean, "This doesn't feel good. I'm stressed."

Pay close attention to your body, especially when you're experiencing conflict with your partner. Your body will tell you when you need to set a boundary.

If you're in the middle of a conversation with your partner, for example, assess how you are feeling inside. If you're cringing, tightening, or bracing, you may want less of something. If you're feeling a deep yearning, missing, or longing, you may want more of something. What do you want? And equally importantly, why do you want it?

ASK, "WHY IS THIS SO IMPORTANT TO ME?"

When setting a boundary, it's important for you to understand what's driving your decision. Rather than proclaiming to your partner "I want more time alone, okay, and that's that!" it's much more productive if you can say, "I want more alone time, and here's why…"

Earlier in this book, we shared this question: "Why is this so important to you?" This is a great question to ask your partner when you're trying to understand their perspective. It's also a great question to flip around and ask yourself!

You want more time alone—why? You want the kitchen to be tidy every day—why? You want permission to use some of your joint savings to invest in a new business idea—why? Try to figure out the deeper reason why you want to have, do, or try something. This "deeper reason" is sometimes called a "core value." A core value is something you cherish and value strongly.

Which of the following things matter to you a great deal? Those things are probably your core values. Which of the following things don't matter to you very much? Those are probably not your core values.

Security	Responsibility	Discipline
Privacy	Passion	Efficiency
Adventure	Loyalty	Health
Self-Expression	Stability	Achievement
Beauty	Family	Freedom
Creativity	Tranquility	Connection
Service/Giving back	Peace	Cleanliness

Honesty	Monogamy	Feeling sexy/sensual
Reliability	Polyamory	Feeling influential
Open-mindedness	Commitment	Feeling understood
Collaboration	Aliveness	Frugality
Drive	Fairness	Affection
Generosity	Harmony	Belonging
Integrity	Kindness	Humor
Playfulness	Realism	Sensitivity

UNDERSTANDING THE CORE VALUE THAT'S BEHIND YOUR DESIRE

Let's say you want more time alone. You feel like you've been spending too much with your partner, and you're craving some room to breathe. "Time alone" is a big desire for you right now. But before you make a big proclamation to your partner about this, start by asking, "Why does this matter to me?"

You could do some journaling and start exploring your thoughts and feelings. You could ask yourself, "What do I value most in life?" And then…aha! Perhaps you realize that "Creativity" is one of your core values. You want to have a life that feels creative—full of self-expression, vibrancy, color, and art. When you're alone, that's when you tend to feel the most creative. Ah, so that's why you've been craving more time alone. It all makes so much sense!

Now, you can make some changes to improve your quality of life. For example, you can decide that every Thursday night is going to be art night—a special evening when you take time alone to work on creative projects instead of hanging out with your partner. You can explain to your partner why having a weekly art night matters so much to you. You can help your partner to understand what's driving your desire for more time alone, so they're not left in the dark, hurt, threatened, or baffled by your choices.

BOUNDARIES MUST BE SPOKEN OUT LOUD

A healthy boundary usually begins with an "I" statement, like, "I want…," I don't want…," "I want more of…," "I want less of…," "I am choosing to…," "I've decided to stop doing…," "I strongly prefer…," or "I'm excited to start doing…"

You can't expect your partner to be a mind reader. That's why it's so important to state your boundary out loud. When you do, you're increasing your intimacy, into-me-see, by sharing more about what's so important to you.

So often, couples mistakenly believe, "Clearly s/he doesn't respect me! If s/he did, s/he never would have…" You think your partner knows what you want and why you want it, but they might not! Your partner is a different human being with different values and different priorities. Even if you have said it once or twice, you may need to remind your partner of your boundary a few more times.

ASK YOUR PARTNER FOR ACCEPTANCE, NOT OBEDIENCE

Once you've shared your boundary aloud, you can ask your partner, "Can you live with that?" or "Can you accept this?" or you could say, "I hope I've done a good job of explaining what I want and why this matters so much to me. I'd like to make some changes. I hope you can accept these changes."

You're not making an ultimatum—"Do this or else!"—but rather, you're stating the change you intend to make in your own life, and you're asking your partner if they can accept this change.

It may be helpful to add, "By the way, you don't have to answer right now. Please take some time and think it over."

Your partner might decide, "Yes, I'm fine with this." Or your partner might realize, "I accept that your values are different from mine. While I don't 'love' the change you're proposing, I can tolerate it, because I can see how much this matters to you."

Regardless of how your partner responds, ultimately, it's up to you to respect your own boundary. Take personal responsibility for creating the life that you want. You want a tidier kitchen? You want a fun morning workout routine? You want to renovate the garage? You want more quiet time alone? You want to feel more energized, sensual, or creative? Take matters into your own capable hands. Determine what you can you do to support your own boundary. It's wonderful when your partner celebrates and supports your boundary—that's ideal, of course—but ultimately, this boundary is about you making changes for you, not demanding that your partner change for you.

COMMON SITUATIONS

During workshops, when we talk about boundaries, our clients often ask the following question:

"But how can I 'take personal responsibility' for my own happiness… when so much of my happiness depends on what my partner decides to do?"

It seems like an impossible conundrum. But here's our philosophy: Even though you're part of a couple, and even though your lives are woven together in many ways, you're still individual people. You're not conjoined twins, connected at the hip. Even if you live together, share finances, and share a home, you're still two separate people. You can still take care of yourself. You can identify what's important to you and why it's important, speak it out loud, and take steps to make sure you're getting what you desire—or at least, more of what you desire.

Again, "personal responsibility" is the key phrase here. For example, if you're feeling lonely and you miss your friends, you can wait passively by your phone, hoping that someone will invite you to do something fun. Or you can take personal responsibility and take action to create what you want. You can host a backyard picnic and invite your friends over! Rather than waiting, wishing, hoping, pleading, or demanding that "other people take care of it," you can take care of things yourself. This is true when it comes to your health, your career, your social circle and friendships, and all parts of your life, including your relationship with your partner.

Take a look at this chart, which outlines some common issues that come up for many couples.

In this chart, we want to show how you can shift from feeling powerless ("She/He has to change") to feeling empowered ("I can make a change").

	Time	Sex	Chores
Issue	My partner is always late leaving the house.	My partner and I don't have as much sex as I would like.	My partner rarely helps out around the house.
"You" statement (not a healthy boundary, because you're demanding that your partner obey or change.)	"You need to be on time!"	"You need to make sex a priority and pay more attention to me!"	"You need to do more work around the house, dammit!"
Core Value (Why this matters so much to you.)	Responsibility	Sexual Aliveness	Cleanliness
"I" statement (healthy boundary, because you're focusing on what you want and how you intend to create this for yourself)	"I want to leave on time."	"I want to feel more sexually alive."	"I want the house to be clean and neat."
Action	"I will let you know when I'm leaving." "I will leave with enough time to get to the location."	"I will self-pleasure more." "I will dress sexy." "I will go out dancing."	"I will hire a housekeeper once a week."

CALVIN AND FIONA'S STORY: SWITCHING FROM "YOU" TO "I"

Calvin and Fiona attended one of our workshops. I, CrisMarie, went over to have a coaching session with them. Calvin kept getting angry because when he would say something to Fiona, Fiona remained quiet. He felt like he wasn't being heard. When I asked him how he felt in his body, he responded, "I get tense, my head hurts, and I feel frustrated."

I asked him to take a stab at stating his boundary. He said to Fiona, "You need to listen to me." I pointed out that he was using a "You" statement rather than an "I" statement. I asked if he could rephrase things, which he did easily: "I want to be heard." Just like that, Calvin expressed a healthy boundary.

"Why is that so important to you?" I asked. He responded, "Because when I was growing up, my mother never listened to me. It's about me feeling respected." Aha! Here, we discovered one of Calvin's core values: Respect.

He asked Fiona, "Can you accept my boundary, 'I want to be heard'?" She replied, "Yes, I get why being heard is important to you. But I don't know how I can help. You're faster than me. Sometimes when you're talking, I'm processing. So I don't say anything. You assume I'm not listening. This isn't always true."

I asked, "Calvin, what can you do to support your boundary?" He looked at me blankly. "I don't know. She needs to hear me."

I had some ideas and asked if he wanted to hear them. He said yes. "After you say something, you can ask Fiona, 'What are you hearing me say?' to see if she caught what you were trying to communicate. You might hear that she's thinking about what you said. Would that help?"

"Absolutely!" Calvin felt much more empowered after identifying what he could do to support his boundary. From that point onward, whenever Calvin and Fiona got into a heated discussion, Calvin would remember to pause occasionally to ask Fiona, "What are you hearing me say?" or "I know I just said a lot of things very fast. Do you want me to wait for a minute so you can process what I just said?" These little micro-pauses made a big difference for both of them. Both Calvin and Fiona felt more respected and understood.

While this worked out beautifully for Calvin and Fiona, we know the boundary-ing process is not always easy.

WHY IS THIS SO HARD?

It can be hard to set boundaries because as we discussed at the beginning of this book, it brings up the tension between being attached in a relationship and being self-differentiated—being your own person.

When you get into relationship, you attach to your partner. You're a unit, a couple. For most people, this brings a felt sense of safety and belonging. However, if you just focus on staying attached, you lose that sense of being your own person. You lose your self-definition, the ME. You know that feeling: "Who am I anyway? I know I'm a good wife and mother or husband and father, but who am *I*?"

When you lose your self-definition, it's a passion-killer in a relationship. Your sexual attraction to each other diminishes. Sure, you may get along really well. You probably rarely even fight. That's because one of you is not showing up as a whole and separate person—or perhaps neither of you are showing up as whole people.

Remember the relationship math that we shared earlier in this book:

1 x 1 = 1 (a whole relationship)

1 x ½ = ½ of a relationship

½ x ½ = ¼ of a relationship

When you don't self-define, meaning you don't share your boundaries about who you are and what you want, there's less of you present in the relationship. Not only does your energy go flat, that flatness is transmitted into the relationship.

Plus, if both of you are only halfway showing up, there's less difference, energy, and spark between you. It's like two magnets that now both have the same energy polarity. The attraction isn't there because the differences are not there.

For a relationship to have a sense of passion, aliveness, and intimacy, both attachment and self-differentiation energies must be present. Yes, you want the sense of relaxation and safety knowing you belong somewhere, the WE. But you also want the sense of being a separate individual, the ME, that feeling of, "I'm my own person with my own choices, rights, and sovereignty."

When one of you decides to speak up, ask for what you want, and set a boundary, then the scale tips—the sense of attachment and belonging is threatened. What if s/he gets mad at me, or even punishes me? What if this ruins everything? What if s/he leaves me?

If you hit this internal resistance and decide not to speak up, you may plummet back into those Opt Out states, in which you feel repressed and your vitality withers. Now you're showing up in your relationship as only half of yourself or a quarter of yourself, and the relationship withers, too.

If you decide it's important enough for you to speak up and state your boundary, well then, you have to cope with the reality that yes, your partner may be upset, the equilibrium of the relationship will be upset, and things will likely change.

That's when you want to apply the tools we talked about in the beginning of this chapter: Breathing, Feeling your Feet and Seat, and Connecting to the Space. These will help you settle yourself and help you tolerate feelings of uncertainty, ambiguity, and discomfort. Sometimes, simply breathing deeply for two minutes can help you remember that no matter what happens next, you can take care of yourself, and you will be okay.

STEPPING TO MY EDGE

Recently, I, CrisMarie, was faced with one of those moments where I needed to state a boundary—but at first, I didn't. Why? Because I felt scared that stating a boundary would lead to painful consequences. Here's what happened…

I was invited to participate in a nine-day training program that would greatly enhance and build upon my coaching practice. I really wanted to sign up for this training. I felt elated about it. However, the dates for the program conflicted with some commitments I had already made—including co-leading a workshop with Susan and taking a trip she'd scheduled for us with her mother.

I immediately said "no" to the training because I figured, "This would never work, and besides Susan would be so upset if I backed out of our teaching gig and the trip with her mom. She'd be furious. It would be so damaging to our relationship." So, that was that; no training for me.

I didn't even bring it up with Susan. As the days rolled along, I found myself quite disappointed. I noticed I was becoming more and more irritable with her. She wondered what was up.

I blurted out (not particularly gracefully, I will admit), "I'm frustrated because I found a training program that I really wanted to do, but the dates conflict with some stuff we've already got on the calendar. I feel annoyed and disappointed. I feel like I always have to lead programs with you, and there's never enough time for me to do things on my own! Right now, I just want to blame you!"

Susan was surprised by my sudden blurt, but she didn't get defensive. Instead, she was curious. She asked me, "Why is this training so important to you?" I told her how the training would help me personally, but also in my coaching practice. I felt relieved just sharing what was important to me.

We talked for quite a while about the impact it would have if I decided to go or if I didn't go. It got quite heated. Both of us were upset during the discussion. She agreed with me that I shouldn't go. She felt like I'd be leaving her in the lurch. This wasn't the first time I'd had a conflict with us leading a program together. We went to bed distant from each other.

Then the next morning while we were having our coffee, Susan said quietly, "I think you should go do the training program." I was stunned. She did have some strong concerns. She would need a co-leader to replace me. She wanted my help finding a suitable replacement. She was disappointed that I wouldn't be traveling with her and her mother, but also was willing to do it alone. I was more than willing to offer my help to find a replacement co-leader.

I'd been certain that if I brought this up, I'd be risking our relationship, because working together is vital to who we are. However, I discovered it didn't threaten our work together. As a matter of fact, taking the nine-day training created much greater clarity for me in my coaching practice, and ultimately, it enhanced our work together.

I learned a great deal from this experience. Ultimately, I learned that even if I think, "I can't say that…I can't do that…no, I can't state that boundary because it will ruin my relationship with Susan, and we'll be doomed for sure!" those fears are not necessarily accurate. It might not "ruin" things at all. It might lead to some temporary conflict and discomfort, sure. But in the long run, stating what I desire makes our relationship better—not worse.

TAKING THE RISK MAKES YOU STRONGER

We have found, time and time again, that when one partner is willing to ask for what they want—possibly threatening the relationship all together—that moment of truth and revelation allows you to stand forward as a whole person, at the edge of your current comfort zone, willing to be seen.

Speaking your truth, rather than making you weaker, actually makes you stronger.

It sounds counterintuitive, but when you take a risk and share what's true for you, you step into an amazingly stable position of strength. In that moment, you are neither leaning on your partner nor holding on to them too tightly. You are standing on your own two feet.

The more you can come to live at the edge of your comfort zone and speak your truth, the more you'll discover that you have the resources to be both alone and fully together as unique individuals. This reveals more room and possibility for individual expression and co-creativity as a couple.

It is scary when you risk speaking your truth, stating who you are and what you want. You assume you know how your partner will react and what the outcome will be. So it can feel like you'll be "causing trouble" or "ending things" if you ask for what you really want. But again, this isn't necessarily the case. We've found if you stay vulnerable and curious in the discussion, you may be surprised at the creative solutions that emerge.

As Mick Jagger says, "You can't always get what you want, but if you try some time, you just might find, you get what you need."

BACK TO YOU

This last section of the book has been about you: the ME. The goal is for you to access more confidence and calmness, as well as discovering more self-clarity—even in the midst of conflict. To do that:

1. Try practicing the tools Breathing, Feel your Feet and Seat, and Connect to the Space, the next time you are stressed—no matter if it's with your partner or not. See if you notice a shift inside yourself, even if it's a small one. The more you practice, the more reward you'll feel when you do this. You'll build your capacity to access more calmness, confidence, creativity, and the ability to think more clearly.

2. Review the recurring issues that come up between you and your partner.

   a. What's something you want very much?

   b. Why is this so important to you? (In other words, what is the underlying core value that is being triggered for you in this area?)

   c. How do you feel in your body when you think about this situation—and what do you think your body is trying to say to you?

4. See if you can create a boundary statement, ideally making this an "I" statement. Make sure it's about you. "I want more…" or "I want less of…" Explain what you want, why you want it, and what you intend to do about it. Remember to focus on changes you can make, rather than demanding that your partner change for you.

5. What can you do to support your boundary? (In other words, how can you take personal responsibility—and individual actions—to create the experiences that you want?)

6. Another good question to consider is: "How could I take my happiness into my own hands? How could I make positive changes that improve my quality of life, even without my partner's involvement?" Hopefully your partner will support you and accept your boundary, but even if they do not...how can you create what you desire, regardless?

CHAPTER 6

The CUE

How to discuss "hot topics"—difficult, sensitive, emotionally charged topics—with your partner in a productive way.

One of the toughest parts of being in a couple is trying to have a conversation about a hot topic—a topic that's tough, sensitive, tricky, delicate, or emotionally charged in some way. When hot topics come up, it's not easy to stay open, curious, and connected. But it is possible!

In this section, we'll give three crucial tips and three powerful tools that will help you handle hot topics more gracefully—tools for listening, discovering, and communicating in ways that will help you build bridges rather than walls.

These three powerful tools are what we think of as the meat and potatoes of communicating well with your partner when hot topics pop up. They are:

1. Committed Reflective Listening

2. *Check It Out!*

3. The 5-5-5

Plus, we want to give you three helpful tips as appetizers before we get to the main course of those powerful tools.

TIPS FOR SUCCESS

TIMING IS IMPORTANT

When do hot topics arise? It's rarely during a perfect, serene moment, like when you're both well rested, fully hydrated, and calmly strolling together hand-in-hand by the seaside! That would be great, but that's typically not how things go. Instead, hot topics tend to arise when you're…

- Both in the bathroom brushing your teeth

- Driving through traffic

- In the kitchen cooking or cleaning

- At the dinner table with kids

- Five minutes away from visiting the in-laws

- Communicating via a text message

There you are brushing your teeth before bed, and your partner says, "By the way, I have to say yes or no to that promotion in Dallas by tomorrow." (You currently happily live in Seattle.) Choking on your toothpaste, you scramble for a reply.

Or your spouse gives you a quick kiss on the cheek while running out the door and telling you, "Oh, I'm not going to be able to make it to the kid's soccer game tonight, the boss called a project meeting." Before you can speak up to discuss your child's disappointment (not to mention your own disappointment), again, your partner is out the door.

Often, hot topics get brought up abruptly—when neither one of you is really prepared!

This is not ideal, but in couples, it happens all the time. It's no wonder these conversations don't go well. Creating the right time and space to have important conversations is vital.

What's the solution? We recommend using common sense before you bring up a hot topic with your partner. If you need to discuss an important (or potentially life-changing) topic, try to choose a moment when you both have some time to actually talk and listen to one another—in other words, not when one of you is dashing out the door. Some couples like to schedule a weekly check-in. They put the time on the calendar—say, one hour, once a week--and if they've got a hot topic to discuss, they'll save it for this timeslot.

Of course, life isn't a computer program. Sometimes schedules need to change or urgent things come up unexpectedly. That's okay. Just try to the best of your abilities not to bring up a hot topic when it's a really inopportune moment. It's just not productive.

RESIST THE URGE TO "FIX IT QUICK"

When a hot topic comes up—whether it's an ideal moment to talk, or a less-than-ideal moment—you might notice that your first instinct is to "fix it quick."

It's natural to go to directly into problem-solving mode. Heck, who likes the uncertainty of not knowing what's going to happen? No one does. So it's natural to think, "What can I do to make this go away and get back to normal life?" And therefore, your impulse is to fix it before even taking the time to listen to each other.

Let's say you're running out the door. You notice that your spouse isn't happy with your manager's decision to call that project meeting right smack in the middle of your child's soccer game. So, you blurt out something, anything, to make it better:

- "Look, I'll make it up to her—promise."

- "This won't keep happening—the big project will be done soon."

- "Let's plan to do a special family event over the weekend. Okay?"

These quick solutions are well-meaning and may even be viable options, but as you blurt out these quick fixes, you're missing the point. You've dropped a bomb on your partner, who wasn't prepared for it. He (or she) is left reeling in the bathroom while you're zipping away without giving your partner a chance to respond or express how they feel. Remember, as adults, we don't need to always get our way, but we do need to feel heard and genuinely considered.

That's why taking the time to listen—and allowing your partner to say how what you've just said impacted them—is a critical part of relating and intimacy.

AVOID THE TRAP OF ASKING QUESTIONS

Because hot topics can often make you feel threatened, some people resort to asking their partners questions rather than sharing their opinion. This seems like a great strategy at the time. When you ask your partner a series of questions, you remain safely hidden, not revealing your beliefs, your wants, or your assumptions; you're just gathering new information.

The problem is you aren't showing up as you. You're not increasing your intimacy—into-me-see. We want to urge you to access your courage and share your real thoughts, feelings, and wants. Yes, your partner may have a reaction. You might have to develop the capacity to tolerate their reactions. You might have to remind yourself that your partner is entitled to be upset and you're not responsible for fixing how they feel.

Plus, when asking questions is overused (as I, CrisMarie, have done over the years), you can end up frustrated, not getting what you want, and thinking you don't matter.

TOOL #1: COMMITTED REFLECTIVE LISTENING

We know it's a challenge to listen, especially when your partner says something you disagree with or something that threatens your world. This happens all the time with couples. And when something threatening comes up, that's the point at which you probably stop listening, and then your mind spins into defenses, explanations, or rebuttals to what seems like an attack. Your body swings into that fight-or-flight stress reaction that we discussed previously. It's so uncomfortable.

But instead of building your next line of defense, imagine listening with your mind and heart open to being changed. We know. This sounds even more threatening, right? You could lose. But what if it isn't about winning or losing? What if it's about remembering this is someone you love and care about, someone who is upset, or has a different point of view than you? Wow. If this were the starting point for listening, most conversations would go very differently!

Actor and screenwriter Alan Alda says:

"Real listening is a willingness to let the other person change you. When I'm willing to let them change me, something happens between us that's more interesting than a pair of dueling monologues."

Don't you love that? When you listen with an open mind and heart, with a real willingness to see another person's point of view, and with a willingness to be "changed" in some way, that's true listening. We call this Committed Reflective Listening.

Let us be clear: we're not necessarily talking about agreeing with your partner. We're talking about taking the time to be interested in how your partner thinks and feels, stepping into their shoes and seeing the world from their point of view.

We find that when couples listen--really listen--to each other, they dramatically increase their connection, goodwill, and creativity in their approach to what can seem like irreconcilable differences. The energy in the conversation shifts. It's palpable. There's a connection to something greater that allows the couple to tap into brilliant options— options that simply hadn't occurred to them before. With committed reflective listening, solutions emerge that neither partner even considered when they were stuck in right/wrong, win/lose, got-to-get-to-the-solution thinking.

Plus, even if the worst-case scenario happens—even if you ultimately decide that whatever conflict you're facing is unsolvable and you break up or get divorced—committed reflective listening makes the break-up process just a little bit calmer. When each person feels that they've been heard and that their position was considered, then both people feel more peace of mind about the break-up and feel more resilient and able to move forward.

Again, we call this committed reflective listening—because indeed, it does take commitment!

So we're not saying it's easy, but we are saying it's a powerful commitment.

REFLECT BACK BEFORE YOU SNAP BACK

When we're working with couples, we often hear one partner saying to the other:

"You never listen to me!"

"I feel like you don't ever hear me!"

We want to acknowledge that it's very difficult to listen and not react when you're talking about topics that are so deeply personal, that involve high stakes, and that may involve big changes in your world.

In those moments, we encourage you to make the commitment to reflect back what you're hearing.

How? It's exactly what it sounds like. First, you allow your partner to complete his/her thought. Then you pause. Then you reflect back what you think you've heard—not every single word they said, just the gist of what your partner said, including their emotional tone. Then you inquire to see if what you're reflecting back matches what they were trying to communicate.

This is a very simple way to calm and settle yourself, listen attentively, and ensure that you're really hearing what your partner is trying to say.

For example, we were coaching Jonathan and Izzy, married for seven years, who were discussing household chores. Izzy brought up her frustration with Jonathan leaving the trash by the door. Jonathan made the commitment to reflect back what he heard before responding, even though he was mad. Here's what he said: "Let me see if I got it. You're frustrated and annoyed that I don't take the trash all the way out to the garbage can. When I leave it by the door, it makes you feel like I don't care about you. Does that fit?"

Izzy visibly relaxed when she heard him. Now, let's be clear: Jonathan didn't agree with Izzy. He did, however, communicate that he really got that Izzy was frustrated and why. Plus, now he knew why his behavior upset her so much—it was because she felt like he didn't care about her.

Too often, people swing right into defending and explaining before really making sure they've received the message that was intended. It sounds so simple, but it really works. Try it—make the commitment to reflect back before you snap back!

TOOL #2: CHECK IT OUT!

Your partner slams the door and you assume, "He's mad at me." That's your assumption. But is it actually true? Maybe. Maybe not! Perhaps your partner's hand slipped and then there was a gust of wind and the door slammed accidentally. Point is, it's impossible to know what's going on inside another person—how they think, feel, or what their motivations are—unless you ask them to share. Only they can confirm what's happening for them on the inside. This is true even if you have lived with your partner for many years. The problem is, we forget this! Most of us make assumptions about our partners all the time, which leads to unnecessary friction.

Not only is your *partner's* internal world not visible to you—you may not even be aware of what's going on inside of *you*. You have a vast internal world made up of what you're wanting, how you're feeling, what you're thinking, and all of the significant emotional life events that have shaped you. All this is swirling around inside of you, which leads you to show up in the way that you do. The same is true for your partner. With all of this, it's hard enough to have a solid grasp on what's going on inside of yourself. It's almost impossible for you to have clarity on what's happening inside your partner,

The first step in relating is to learn to build a bridge to yourself, to your own internal world, so you can understand how you are putting the pieces together. It takes vulnerability to take this step—to identify and then reveal what's happening inside of you.

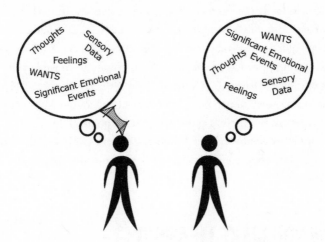

The second step in relating is to build a bridge to your partner, so they can have some room to show up as themselves, versus what you're projecting onto them or assuming about them. This takes curiosity and the willingness to listen, allowing them to reveal how they put the pieces together.

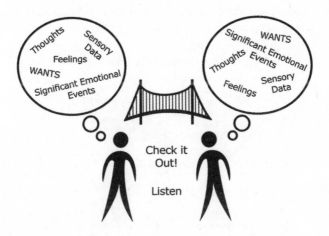

There's a tool for this, which we call *Check It Out!*

This tool is really the foundation of communicating effectively with your partner in tough situations. To make sure you really get it, we're going to first talk about how we as humans process (or how we make meaning), which will help you break things down when you want to use the *Check It Out!* tool. The way we make meaning feels automatic to most human beings because it happens quickly and often unconsciously. But there is actually quite a lot going on internally when we process information. When you understand how your brain makes assumptions, communicating becomes much easier. Here's how it works:

HOW YOU MAKE MEANING

As a human being, you attach meaning to what you hear, see, and experience. It's natural. The brain is a meaning-making machine. You make sense of the world through the data you take in and sort the data through your personal filter. Then you create a story, which drives how you feel. Just remember, everyone processes incoming information differently. Let's take a look at the five things that happen when humans make meaning:

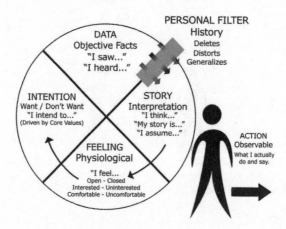

How Humans Process

DATA

You receive information or data through your senses: what you hear, see, taste, touch, and smell. Data is objective information with no meaning attached. For example: I see my partner is crying and sad. This is not objective data. If I am truly objective, the more accurate statement is that I see CrisMarie has tears on her cheeks, or stated even more objectively, I see she has water on her cheeks. I don't know how she feels. Maybe she has allergies, or maybe she has an eyelash in her eye. These are all viable alternative meanings.

PERSONAL FILTER

You take in data, and it is processed through your own personal filter. Your personal filter is made up of all that makes you unique: gender, age, where you grew up, past relationship history, and your significant emotional life events. Your brain sorts the data, labeling some things good and other things bad. You do this unconsciously.

Say, for example, when you were young, a small dog bit you. Ever since then, you've been afraid of small dogs. Your brain and nervous system now categorize all small dogs as dangerous. Today, when you see a small dog, you immediately feel fear. For someone else, seeing a small dog might elicit a completely opposite or even neutral reaction.

As the information or data goes through your personal filter, your brain deletes, distorts, and generalizes information. That's why you and your partner can have such different interpretations of the same event or conversation.

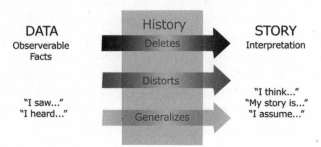

YOUR STORY

Data goes through your personal filter and out pops your story. Your story is your interpretation, hunch, opinion, assumption, theory, or judgment of the situation. Remember, we use the word "story" to emphasize that you are making things up as you go. Your experience may strongly reinforce your story, but it's still your story just the same. Here are some examples:

"Joe doesn't think I'm attractive." This is a story, not a fact. The data you've collected may lead you to this conclusion (he has stopped touching you, he didn't say anything when you walked in with a new hairstyle, and he doesn't initiate sex very often), but still, it's only your story.

"My partner does not want to go back to work!" Maybe you can point to pieces of data that lead you to this conclusion: he's spending lots of time hiking, biking, and playing with the kids. Still, it's just a story. You don't know how your partner is feeling. (Remember Mary and Tom—there was more to why Tom wasn't actively looking for work.)

It's critical to notice that your story is something that's been created inside your own mind and that it's not necessarily true. And it's important to know that your stories drive your feelings.

YOUR FEELINGS

You generate feelings from the stories you tell yourself. Feelings come in four major categories: happy, sad, mad, or scared. There are many variations on these four emotional themes, and we've made it simpler by reducing it to two categories: emotions that feel like you're opening up to your partner (warm/connected), and emotions that feel like you're closing down (cold/distant).

Emotions are energy in your body. Similar to how the waves of the ocean ebb and flow, when you respond to something at a feeling level, you are either opening to it or closing off to it; moving towards it or away from it. At the physiological level, this can register as temperature change, warm or cold; or it can be a sense of the distance between you and your partner, closer or farther. So, you can feel close to your partner or distant from them, or warm or cold towards them.

Feelings Are Psychological

Another way of thinking about emotions is related to your physical position relative to your partner or their idea. Are you leaning forward and interested, or are you leaning back, crossing your arms and disinterested?

Let's experiment.

Start by bringing to mind something about your partner of which you are fond. Maybe it's their smile, their laugh, or the way it feels when you're cuddling. What happens in your body? Do you open and soften? Do you feel warm? Do you notice yourself leaning forward?

Now think of something that you don't like or a recent interaction that didn't go well. What shifts in your body? Do you tighten or brace anywhere in your body? Do you get colder or notice a desire to back up or turn away?

This exercise helps you notice your own internal landscape. Everyone has their own unique physiological reactions. We encourage you to bring your awareness to how you feel in your body when you experience positive or negative events in your day.

INTENTION

From your feelings, you generate your intention. Your intentions reflect your desires, your wishes, and what you want. They link to your core values, which we brought up when we were talking about boundaries.

When you're communicating with your partner, you can have more than one intention at any one time.

For example, you're dealing with planning a vacation. One intention might be getting to a warmer climate during the winter months, and another could be that you're worried about spending too much money and you want to save more.

You may even notice your intentions shifting in the moment. You may start with an intention to listen to your partner, but as you hear them tell their side of the experience, you realize your intention is not to listen, but to defend your position.

It's important to check in regularly with yourself and notice your own shifting thoughts, feelings, and intentions.

As a meaning-making machine, recognize that you constantly sort data through your senses and you attach your own meaning to the data. That generates how you feel. You cannot stop the data from coming in. Your brain is wired to receive it and translate it. We suggest that you be aware of the stories you tell yourself and consider that you may not be right. Make a point to *Check It Out!*.

Checking out your story with your partner is the key to creating healthy dialogue. It's helpful to start with data, then share your story as a story, even your feelings, and *Check It Out!*

Check Out Your Story!

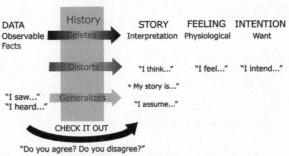

To illustrate, we'll share an experience we had with Nancy and Jay.

Nancy and Jay were doing couples coaching with us over video chat. They were struggling with some important decisions about next steps for their family and career. They'd met in business school while getting their MBAs over fifteen years before. Now they were married with two children, ages eight and six. Both Nancy and Jay loved having kids. In many ways, their life seemed quite ideal.

The big decision was whether Nancy should take on a new leadership role at work that might demand much more of her time and energy. Nancy had slowed her career down when the kids were very young. But she loved working and had been encouraged by her boss to take over a new business line she'd been instrumental in starting. While Jay said he was okay with stepping up more at home, something seemed unspoken.

In one of the coaching sessions, Nancy started to talk about the new responsibilities she'd have. "This is a huge opportunity for our company, but it's also risky. If it goes well, though, the new business line will probably pave the way for an IPO. I'm so excited! When I'm not busy being terrified, that is."

Jay cut in, "Okay, wait. Let's get back to reality. Any chance of an IPO is a longshot, right?" Jay knew a bit about IPOs. He was in project management at a local company, which allowed him the freedom to move from one project to another, make a solid paycheck, and not have to deal with company politics.

Nancy responded, "No, not really. Even before this new business line, the company has always wanted to go public if possible."

"But this will be a huge time commitment. I could support a new position but not going through an IPO. You'll be gone all the time!" Suddenly Jay sounded defensive.

I, Susan, interjected, I started with my intention, "Let's slow this down." Next, I shared some data, "You'd been very keen and supportive, Jay. Then you shifted." Now my story, "Maybe it's the new information about the IPO, but I'm thinking something else is bothering you." Finally, I checked it out. "I want to check—is something else up?"

Jay responded quickly, "No." Then he took a breath and said, "It's just that, right this second when she mentioned the IPO, it really hit me how this promotion might change our lives. I don't like it."

Nancy jumped in, "Come on, Jay! You knew I wanted to focus on my career now." With some coaching, she paused, "Let me start again. (Intention) I hear you saying this promotion might change our lives. (Data) I'm feeling like you don't want me to step into a leadership role. I'm even wondering if you don't want me working full-time. But maybe that's just my assumption and it's not true? I don't know. (Story) I'm frustrated (Feeling), because I've worked hard for this! I want to check in with you. Can you share more about what you're feeling?" (*Check It Out!*)

A longer pause this time, and then Jay said:

"No—I want you to work and be successful. It's not the time, or hell, even the IPO." Jay was visibly uncomfortable. "I didn't anticipate…" Jay looked down and mumbled, "I would feel threatened." There it was, Jay was vulnerable and beginning to touch on what was really up for him.

He continued, "I've never been as motivated to get to the top as you. I'm happy with my work. But if all this goes well—man, you'll be the big breadwinner. I think I am anxious about that. What if I'm not enough?"

Nancy was surprised, and responded, "I had no idea you felt like that. I want to hear more about how you are feeling about this—it doesn't mean I won't take the next career step, but for me, it's important that we keep talking about this and share what the impact is for both of us."

The conversation shifted. It was much more real and honest about what was happening underneath the situation.

Taking the time to break it down: intention, data, story, feeling, and then explicitly checking out your story—is a way to share how you put the world together and see what fits with your partner. It's about slowing things down and really understanding both yourself and the other.

We want to encourage you to use your vulnerability and curiosity to break it down and check out your stories with your partner. You will discover things you wouldn't learn otherwise. It's impossible to know how someone thinks or feels or what their motivations are unless you explicitly check out your story and hear it from him or her.

So, the next time you notice yourself making an assumption about your partner—"He thinks I'm unattractive," "She never considers my feelings," "He always prioritizes work over me!" "She's trying to control me"—rather than automatically believing this assumption, check and see if it's actually true. It's possible that your partner has no idea they've been impacting you in this way. Give them a fair chance to explain their true feelings and intentions. Open yourself up to the possibility that maybe your assumption was incorrect.

Again, we call this communication tool *Check It Out!*, because that's exactly what you're doing. When you notice yourself making an assumption, judgment, or interpretation, rather than automatically believing your own thoughts, you *Check It Out!*. You ask your partner if they agree or disagree. You check and see. This is such a simple practice, but it really shifts the energy between you and your partner, enabling you to bridge differences, build trust, and deepen intimacy.

HOT TOPICS!

Hot topics can come up and escalate quickly when you least expect them to. We want to provide you one more surefire tool to tackle these tough topics.

TOOL #3: THE: 5-5-5

We've saved the best tool for last, because this is truly one of our favorites!

With hot topics, it can be like matches starting a fire. Each of you is so sensitive that you react quickly, jumping in to defend or to interrupt, going back and forth, and ultimately getting nowhere and feeling miserable. When you come upon a topic that regularly escalates for your couple, like: sex, money, the kids, the in-laws, or who takes out the garbage, intervene with a 5-5-5.

A 5-5-5 is designed to create clear boundaries, providing time and space for each person to be heard, while also creating a container that provides a beginning, middle, and end to the conversation. It might not be enough time to solve the problem, but it's a good start!

A 5-5-5 allows each of you to uncover for yourself why this topic is so important to you and what core values are driving your urgency or importance on the matter. In other words: why you care so darn much about this.

So let's talk about how to do a 5-5-5!

First, find the time and space to have a conversation without outside interruption. This does *not* mean several hours. We're talking small. It's only fifteen minutes. Yep, just fifteen minutes—that's it. Even if you're very busy people, we're confident that both of you can set aside fifteen minutes to invest in your relationship.

Second, figure out who's going to go first. Just flip a coin if you are having trouble deciding.

1. For the first five minutes: Person A talks about the issue. Person B listens, does not interrupt, and tries not to react.

2. For the second five minutes: Reverse it. Person B talks about the issue from their point of view, and Person A listens as neutrally as possible.

3. For the third five minutes: You engage in a dialogue together.

Five minutes can seem like a long time for some. It doesn't mean you need to talk nonstop, but that five minutes is yours to have the space to reflect and say what you need to say on the topic. To some, this may seem lengthy, but for others, it gives ample time to think out loud and speak without being interrupted.

Let's look at an example.

Meet Cindy and Steve. They've been married 25 years and have two kids, as well as a successful national branding and web design company. We were doing regular couples coaching with them, and when they showed up for our session, this is the story they told us.

Apparently, Cindy started it. "We don't have enough long-term savings. We have to save more." Cindy brought up this hot topic while driving home from their accountant's office. It wasn't the first time she had tried to broach this sensitive subject.

"Geez, we're doing the best we can with the business right now," Steve replied as he drove the truck down the road.

"But I can't stand to see how little we put away each year. When I had my corporate job in San Francisco, I was able to save so much more. Plus, my employer matched it, and I could see it growing so fast," Cindy lamented, her voice full of regret.

"Listen, I am doing the best I can! I am not some big corporation, you know," Steve responded, and started to speed up while going around the curves.

"Whoa! Slow down. There are deer on the roads this time of night. You're going to get us killed!" Cindy grabbed the handle above the door.

"Stop telling me how to drive! You are so controlling! I'm fifty-one, and I know how to drive a frickin' truck!" Steve snapped.

"I am not controlling!" Cindy turned and stared out the window.

They drove on in steaming silence.

Cindy crossed her arms and looked straight ahead. "Fine. Never mind. It is clear you don't care about what is important to me."

Sound familiar? Maybe not the content or the roles, but whenever there's a hot topic being discussed, it's amazing how quickly things can escalate from "normal conversation" to "car swerving out of control." To prevent this kind of escalation from happening, we recommend using a 5-5-5.

When Cindy and Steve did the 5-5-5, during Cindy's five minutes, she realized that the reason she was so worried was because two other couples close to them were struggling financially due to unexpected health crises. Cindy saw what tremendous pressure it was putting on both of those relationships. She did not want that to happen to her and Steve. Without taking time for a 5-5-5, the underlying issue would not have surfaced, and they'd probably still be fighting about Steve's driving.

For me, CrisMarie, the 5-5-5 tool is important because it ensures that I'll be able to speak for a while without being interrupted. Having a full five minutes gives me permission to keep going and to find the courage to say what's really true for me.

For me, Susan, this was a relationship saving tool. CrisMarie has always been, and still is, reluctant to take vacations. She doesn't like to be away from work for fear of missing an opportunity. A few years back, I finally got her to take a yoga retreat vacation with me. I was so excited. We arrived and were unpacking our things in our beautiful open-air palapa with a view of the ocean. That's when CrisMarie turned to me and said, "I'm not happy in this relationship."

WTF!?! Not only was I blindsided, but I was crushed. Really? We were finally on vacation, and now we were going to have to spend all our time processing the angst of our relationship!

So I suggested, "What if each day we do a 5-5-5 in the morning about our relationship and then go on to enjoy our yoga retreat?" CrisMarie was suspicious about whether this would be enough time to work things out, but agreed to try it… as long as she could add an additional 5-5-5 at the end of the day if she felt like she needed it. That worked for me.

The result: I discovered that there were a number of things related to our business together that CrisMarie believed she was doing alone. I had no idea that she was wanting something different. She also identified a strong desire to do more theater, as she missed performing onstage and realized that she'd been stopping herself from returning to it. She'd been assuming (incorrectly) that I wouldn't be happy if she took more time to audition and perform in local theater productions. By doing a 5-5-5 every morning, we discovered so much about each other and we each felt heard and considered, and eventually, we were able to brainstorm some great solutions. 5-5-5 saved our vacation, and more importantly, our relationship!

TIPS FOR 5-5-5 SUCCESS

- When using the 5-5-5- tool, don't expect to resolve the issue in one sitting. You might, or you might not. The main goal is to speak, listen, and try to understand each other, rather than leaping right into problem-solving.

- Use a timer, and stop when the timer goes off—no exceptions. Yep, even if you're in the middle of a sentence, even if you aren't done with making your point.

- After the 15 minutes are up, end the discussion. Do not carry on. Give yourself a break from it and do something else. Really.

- If this is a tough recurring issue, you may want to do a weekly or daily 5-5-5 on the topic.

IN SUMMARY

We covered a lot in this chapter. Give yourself a pat on the back. You got through this material! The good news is that these three tips and three tools are the crown jewels of communicating effectively with your partner when hot topics pop up. In fact, they are so important that we want to give you a quick summary here for reference to help you remember.

The three tips are:

- Timing is Important
- Resist the Urge to "Fix It Quick"
- Avoid the Trap of Asking Questions

The three tools are:

- Committed Reflective Listening
- *Check It Out!*
- The 5-5-5

Finally, please don't expect it to be easy. You're talking about hot topics. Remember to use the tools from Chapter 5 (the ME) to settle yourself during these conversations. Know that it takes practice, you will get better at it, and it's a process. Even Susan and I have tense moments when something comes up that is really important for both of us. Heck, we're human. So are you.

BACK TO YOU

Think of a hot topic that either came up recently, or that comes up repeatedly in your relationship. Maybe not the hottest topic, but one that feels moderately challenging.

Try out Committed Reflective Listening. You can use it even when the situation isn't tense. Pause and take in what your partner is saying, and before you share your opinion, make the commitment to reflect back what you're hearing, the gist of the content as well as the emotional tone.

What is the story you're telling yourself about what's happening? Are you making some assumptions, judgments, or interpretations about what your partner is feeling or what his/her intentions might be?

Could you take one of those assumptions and use the *Check It Out!* tool? Can you check and see if your assumption is actually true?

Ask your partner if they're willing to do a 5-5-5 on one of your recurrent issues. Again, don't pick the toughest one. After doing the 5-5-5, what did you learn about yourself? Your partner? The issue?

CHAPTER 7

The Situation

Exploring the problem or dilemma that you're trying to solve—with curiosity— and finding creative solutions.

The Situation is the context that you and your partner are dealing with—the problem you are trying to solve, the recurring issue, the dilemma you're facing, whatever issue is causing you to experiencing conflict.

The Situation could be whether you move to a new city because of your partner's job, how to handle your spouse's serious health issue, your troubled child, recovering (or not) from an affair, or something else.

The Situation also includes the stage of your relationship—for instance, are you newly together or thirty years in, living separately or living together, children or no children, starting careers or retiring?

In this section, we'll talk about what to do when you're caught in tough, angst-producing situations or what can seem like "irreconcilable differences." We'll show you how to apply the tools we've shared previously. We'll give you some rules of the road to help you through these toughest of issues. We'll give you a healthy way to deal with anger. We'll also talk about how different couples have handled issues like affairs, open relationships, and other tough situations.

We'll finish with some guidance on how to build agreements together—agreements that help both of you to continue communicating openly. These are crucial for dealing with hot topics in supportive ways.

WE CAN'T TALK ABOUT THIS

When couples come to our workshops—either in Montana or up at The Haven—they often say to us, "We can't talk about this."

"This" can be anything from an affair to issues with their kids, religious or political differences, or some type of addiction. It can feel too difficult for one or both of them to talk about.

Why is it so difficult to talk about? Some people (and couples) interpret their issues as unmentionable, too weird, too awful, or too different. They may feel too much shame. They may assume that nobody else will really understand. This keeps the topic hidden and secret rather than seen in the light of day and discussed. But when it's brought into the light, new information, honest dialogue, and deeper intimacy can occur.

In one of our couples programs, we were coaching two different couples who were working through the challenges of a polyamorous relationship—or as the second couple referred to it, an "open relationship." These couples would talk to CrisMarie and I privately, but they didn't want to share their struggles with the other couples in the group. They worried the other couples wouldn't "get it" or might shun them. However, during our four days together, gradually these couples opened up. Rather than being shunned, they were embraced with great empathy. Both of these couples discovered that there was great value in revealing their struggles versus staying silent.

We aren't saying it's easy to talk about these tough issues, but talking is the way through. Perhaps you've been taught that you shouldn't talk about sex, money, or politics. But really—if you're going to be in an intimate, healthy relationship, you'd better be talking about those topics!

You may be sitting there thinking your relationship is broken beyond all hope of repair. But then when you hear the issues that other couples are struggling with, you realize, "Wow, everyone faces challenges. I can relate. We're not so different." After an openhearted dinner conversation with friends, or a group therapy session, or a group couples program like the ones that we run, you walk away feeling like, "We're not crazy. We're pretty normal." This puts you into a very different mindset. It's so powerful to recognize, "We are not alone in this struggle."

IRRECONCILABLE DIFFERENCES

All couples bump into issues where they don't align. It can feel quite threatening—like there is absolutely no way through this. Here are several issues that we've encountered working with couples that can, initially, feel like irreconcilable differences…although, they don't necessarily have to be:

- *Religion*: You're a Buddhist. He's Mormon. How will we raise the kids?

- *Where to live*: She gets her dream job in New York City and is ecstatic, but you hate Manhattan. What to do?

- *Mental illness*: He struggles with extreme depression, suicidal thoughts, and/or addictions. You obviously want to help him get well, but what if he never does? Should you stay together and accept that this is just how it is?

- *Gender expression*: One partner realizes, "I'm transgender, and I want to start living/dressing as a woman"—and you support them but also don't feel attracted to them anymore. Now what?

- *Polyamory vs. Monogamy*: You want to try polyamory, but your partner is very threatened and wants to stay monogamous. Is there any hope of staying together?

- *Other major physical changes*: One partner gains 200 pounds… or there's some other dramatic physical change that you don't find appealing. Now what?

- *Sexual kinks*: You have a kink that your wife finds repulsive. You wish she was into it, but she's just not!

- *Major differences in terms of lifestyle preferences*: You like to take uber-long-distance hikes, like traversing the Pacific Coast Trail, which requires months of grueling training and three or four months to hike. Meanwhile, your partner has a traditional nine-to-five job and misses you terribly when you're gone. Of course your partner wants you to be happy and pursue your passions, however, s/he doesn't enjoy having you gone so long.

These are difficult situations. We're not going to unpack and solve them in this chapter—that would be missing the point. Plus, it would be way too long. Instead, we're going to show you how to open the door to dialogue, because remember, this is not about solving the problem. It's about finding ways to live, love, relate, and create through the differences, even the big ones. We do want you to know, though, that the tools can work for any and all of these situations.

Don't get us wrong. We're not saying that you can always work your way through everything and stay happily together. What we're saying is, there are some key tips here to help you maintain a healthy connection—and even deepen your intimacy—while you work through the issue. There are tools to get to the root of the issue. And, you may surprise yourself and come up with solutions you didn't even think were possible.

We've found when couples slow down, listen to each other, and really get underneath what's driving them both, surprising possibilities emerge for their situation.

THE RULES OF THE ROAD

Previously in this book, we shared several tools to help you communicate more successfully—especially when discussing hot, emotionally charged topics. Now, we'll share a few more suggestions and tools that you can use when discussing your Situation.

TIP #1. SLOW DOWN. DON'T RUSH TO A SOLUTION.

The first tip is: don't rush to a solution. Too often, couples want to figure out the answer to their Situation RIGHT NOW before they have adequately addressed the ME and the WE (review those earlier sections of this book if you need a refresher course on what these terms mean).

It is your discomfort with hanging out in uncertainty, as well as the tension and ambiguity of not having a solution, that drives you to want to get to "the answer." It's hard, but it's important to learn how to tolerate being in a state of not knowing. It's the uncertainty that actually is the key to accessing your creativity.

Yes, it's uncomfortable. You're probably not good at it, but it's critical if you're going to solve the real issue. Too often what seems like the right or only answer...

- "We can't raise the kids with any religion since we are so different."

- "I have to move to NYC, even though I hate it, to be with you."

- "You need to lose weight if we're going to stay together."

...doesn't address the underlying issue.

When you are attempting to tackle these sensitive issues, slow down and give yourself time to really digest what is happening. Otherwise, you'll often be solving the wrong issue. Often what is presenting at the surface masks what's driving each of you underneath. You need to take time to unravel the real issue for both of you. So again, don't rush to a solution.

To help uncover what's motivating each of you, we recommend using the tool we talked about in Chapter 6: the 5-5-5. That's where one person speaks openly (uninterrupted) for five minutes, then the other person speaks for five minutes, and then you have a discussion together for five minutes. You may even want to do repeated 5-5-5s on the topic over time, because your Situation may have more nuances than either of you initially think. Doing 5-5-5s allows you to peel back the layers and discover what's driving you and what's driving your partner.

We also suggest that you use the *Check It Out!* tool that we shared in Chapter 6 when approaching these tough topics. Check out your assumptions and see if they're actually true.

Finally, it's always helpful to use committed reflective listening, which we also discussed in Chapter 6. There are a few other tools that may help, too, but those three tools are great places to start.

TIP #2. ASK, "WHY IS THIS SO IMPORTANT TO ME?"

This is a crucial question to uncover what's going on inside of you. When you take time to inquire within about what's underneath this issue for you—and what core value is being triggered—you'll be addressing the issue at the right level. Take some time to consider the Situation and investigate for yourself:

- "Why is this so important to me?"
- "What is the core value that's driving me to want what I want?"

This will help you unearth what the real issue is for you.

If you don't take the time to investigate what the issue is about for you at a deep level, you may only show up with half of yourself, you may agree to do something you will later resent, or you may make a hasty decision and then regret it. Discovering why is this so important to you and voicing it is crucial for you to feel whole. Yes, even if it doesn't fit for your partner.

TIP #3. ASK, "WHY IS THIS SO IMPORTANT FOR YOU?"

When you find yourself at loggerheads with your partner—"You're wrong. I'm right!" or "How can you want that?!"—or when you're feeling like you can't win or aren't being heard, again, slow down. Stop trying to make your point. Stop trying to rush to a solution. Breathe deeply and ask, "Why is this so important to you?" With this question, you're encouraging your partner to go deeper, discover, and articulate for themselves what the core value is that is needing to be addressed.

Consider, why would this person you love and care about have such a different point of view on this topic? Here's your chance to commit to listening to and being curious about your partner. You don't need to agree with them or defend your position. See if you can simply take in how your partner puts their world together. Here are a few examples:

TRINA AND WES: KIDS

Both Trina and Wes wanted kids but had careers that kept being more important. When they married eight years ago, Trina had just graduated with her MBA and agreed to support Wes through law school. After law school, the topic of kids came up, but Trina was really enjoying her job. They each believed kids needed a stay-at-home parent in order to thrive, and she was not ready to leave work.

Now, Trina was thirty-three, a rising star at her technology company, and had just been offered a big opportunity to open and lead a new operation, which would take a couple of years to solidify.

The topic of kids came up again, and they were stalled. When I, CrisMarie came over to coach them, I asked Trina, "Why is it so important for you to take this promotion?" She replied, "I absolutely love my job. I feel so alive. Plus, this company really treats me well. I feel like this is what I'm meant to do."

Then I turned and asked Wes, "Why is it so important to you that she have kids now?" Wes blurted out, "I've already told her, I've wanted kids from the beginning, and she keeps stalling."

I responded, "Okay, really check in. Why is this so important to you, Wes?" He paused, "Well, I don't know if I've ever really admitted this, but I don't want one or two kids…I'd like three or five."

"What?!" Trina exclaimed, "You've got to be kidding. I don't want to be a stay-at-home mom and pop out babies for you. Jeez, you just want me barefoot and pregnant in the kitchen!" She crossed her arms and turned away.

Wes leaned forward and continued, "Whoa, that's not it at all! I want you to have your career." Tina turned to look at him, and Wes continued, "You know I come from a family of seven kids, and I loved growing up that way. I still like hanging out with my brothers and sisters. I want our kids to have that experience too. If we don't start having kids now, I'm afraid it won't happen."

I interjected, "So Wes, you're okay with Trina keeping her career?" Trina interrupted, "Well, who's going to take care of all those kids?!"

"Now, that's an interesting question to ask, and one you can talk about," I smiled. Wes and Trina had apparently never thought of Wes staying home to take care of the kids. It was a possible solution they hadn't even yet considered.

CINDY AND ROD: GUNS

Cindy and Rod had been together for fifteen years and had two kids, ages ten and thirteen. They came to our Couples Mojo retreat because they were lacking passion and aliveness. Through the various stages of their relationship—from romance to having a family and making career choices—they'd had good communication, which helped them successfully get through their challenges. However, there was one topic they simply couldn't talk about: guns and having a gun in the home.

Rod, who was a police officer and kept his revolver at work, wanted to have a gun at home. Over the years, every time he broached the topic, Cindy would go quiet, get up, and walk away, saying, "We're not talking about this." For Cindy, she had a bottom line: *no guns* in the house.

For Rod, the issue was surfacing again because he wanted to teach the kids how to use a gun. He brought it up at the Couples Mojo workshop. When he did, Cindy shut down and was about to walk out of the room. Rod waved me (Susan) over.

When I got there and was up to speed, I encouraged Cindy to explore her resistance. She looked at me with steel in her eyes. I reminded her, "You spoke the first night about a lack of passion and aliveness in your relationship, right?" She slowly nodded. I continued, "This is the first area of real conflict to come up for you two since the start of the workshop. I would invite you to try a 5-5-5 on the topic of guns in the house, answering for each of you: why is this so important to you?"

Cindy reluctantly agreed and went first. She spoke of her kids' safety; her belief in gun control; that guns were bad. No way was she going to have guns in her house. There was no way she was going to change her mind.

What surprised her was that when Rod spoke, he also spoke of his kids' safety. His belief was that learning how to respect and handle a gun was the best way to ensure his kids' safety. He thought they were still too young, but he wanted to be able to educate them. Rod also shared how he had felt shut out and disrespected each time Cindy refused to talk about the topic.

For Cindy, this was a humbling experience. She acknowledged her self-righteous position on guns and her obliviousness to how her refusal to talk had impacted Rod. This unlocked the door to more open communication. It also led to more passion between them. It wasn't about the decision about guns or no guns. It was about embracing the edges of their differences and discovering what mattered to each other and why. This was new and exciting.

ELLEN AND GARY: PORNOGRAPHY AND LYING

Ellen and Gary had been married for eight years and had two kids, ages two and five. Both Ellen and Gary work in San Francisco. Between the demands of work, long commutes, and the kids, they'd had little time for each other. Over the previous nine months, Gary'd had extra stress at work due to a big project. He was getting home so late that Ellen and the kids had often gone to bed by then.

Gary uses pornography to de-stress. Early in the relationship, Gary shared his pornography use with Ellen. While Ellen didn't love it, she agreed it was okay. When the children came, they agreed that Gary would not use pornography at home. He agreed if the need came up, he'd talk to Ellen about it first.

They arrived at our couples program because Ellen had caught Gary using porn late in the evening. He admitted he'd been doing it for the last couple of months. She was furious and had asked him to go stay with one of his friends.

I [Susan] came over to coach them and ventured to Ellen, "Can you tell Gary why it's so important to you that he doesn't use porn at home?"

Ellen answered, "To be honest, it's not that you are using porn. Sure, I don't like it, and I have some concerns, which we can talk about." Then she became teary, adding, "But what really hurts is you didn't tell me. You lied to me, and you've been lying to me for months! We agreed you'd tell me. You promised you would. Now, I don't trust you!"

Gary's head dropped; he paused. When he spoke, it was almost a whisper, "I couldn't tell you. I was too ashamed." He got choked up and went on, "I don't want to use porn in our home with the kids there. I couldn't stop myself, and I didn't want to admit it."

Ellen was visibly relieved and touched to hear Gary acknowledge what had been going on for him. She replied, "Look, Gary, for me, this really isn't about the pornography. It is about you lying. We could have worked on a solution, but you didn't give me the chance."

Did this single conversation fix the Situation? No. But it did open the door to the real issue, and to honest dialogue, intimacy, and connection. This is the path to rebuilding.

In each of the examples that we just shared, there's no final answer. They are each a work in progress. Again, a tough Situation is rarely resolved in a single conversation. However, one honest conversation can open the door to seeing yourself and your partner more deeply. This creates a stronger sense of intimacy. The energy between the two human beings in the couple shifts dramatically from tight, righteous, and defensive to open, curious, and loving. As a result, many more creative options open up to you. If you can keep from rushing to a solution, you may come up with a unique solution, or at the very least, you may feel quite differently about the decision you do make.

TIP #4. ACKNOWLEDGE RATHER THAN APOLOGIZING

When your partner is upset with you, it's so tempting to apologize and promise you'll never do it again. "I'm sorry. It won't happen again. I swear." These apologies and promises are often hollow. It may feel like the right thing to say in the moment, but it's usually motivated by the desire to make the tension go away as fast as possible. It's a flimsy Band-Aid, not a solution.

A common issue that comes up in our couples workshops is one partner having had an affair. This is such a tough issue for couples. Trust can be broken. The safety of the relationship is rattled. The good news is, it may be rattled so much that both partners become much more open and honest about how they've felt and what wasn't working for them. This allows for everything to be put on the table to be discussed. This raw honesty is freeing for the individual and powerful for the relationship.

TINA AND STEVE: AN AFFAIR

Tina and Steve, both in their fifties and in their second marriage, had been together for twelve years. When they met, Tina was a manager at her father's manufacturing company. Steve was a travel writer and Tina's great white knight, having traveled the globe. Nine years into their relationship, Tina's father passed away and she took over the business. Her job became a big one—leading a group of men, going to conferences, and working with business consultants to improve the business.

They showed up at our workshop after Steve had an affair.

Tina was clearly hurt and angry. When I, Susan, went over to coach them, Steve was apologizing. "It was just a dumb move on my part. I'm sorry. Please believe me. It won't happen again."

I spoke up, "I believe you mean that right now, Steve. The only problem is there's no acknowledgment of what went on beforehand and what caused you to initiate the affair."

Steve reiterated, "I was just stupid."

I tried again, sharing one possible perspective. "I imagine with Tina's new job and bigger world, you might have felt replaced and less important. Does any of that fit?"

Steve flatly denied it, saying, "No way. I'm fine. I love her. It was a onetime thing. It won't happen again."

It would have felt very different if Steve, rather than apologizing to Tina, had said something like, "I get it. You're hurt and angry. You have every right to be. I was used to being the strong one, the one you turned to, the guy you leaned on. Now, you have all these other men and people around. My career is stalling, and yours is taking off. I feel jealous and not important."

If he had acknowledged what was really going on for him, it might have made an impact on Tina. Plus, he may have been able to listen to how it was for Tina—without trying to fix it.

Steve didn't. As a result, it cost him his relationship. They divorced.

When you do acknowledge what is or was going on for you and what you did, you're taking responsibility for your actions. This may or may not help in the relationship dynamic. It does, however, help you, because you're being congruent and honest with yourself. No more hiding, denying, or apologizing. This is quite powerful.

When you acknowledge what has happened, you're also acknowledging the impact your actions have had on your partner. This gives your partner a chance to be seen and heard for how it is (or was) for them when you behaved that way. This is the path to possible rebuilding.

HOW TO WORK WITH ANGER

In Chapter 5 (the ME) we talked about shifting from reacting to responding. We gave you tools to settle your nervous system. It may seem as though we think reacting is not healthy or helpful. That's not the case.

Reactivity is a very normal, healthy, and even a vital aspect of the human wiring. It's your reptilian brain letting you know there's danger and you need to move fast. In our view, it's not about getting rid of your reaction, but more about how to use your reaction as a choice and pathway for creating more intimacy—into-me-see.

When things are heating up between you and your spouse, when you have strong differences, when you have radically different core values that are clashing, strong emotions and reactions are natural.

Part of our reactive system is feeling angry. Anger is a normal emotion and a healthy energetic reaction. It's normal to feel angry when you interpret that someone has crossed your boundary—bumped into you in an energetic way. Too many people suppress their anger, and then it squirts out in unproductive ways, or the energy goes inward, which can result in you getting sick.

When you are reacting with anger, you have a choice: either just blow up and clean up the damage later (or not), or share your reaction with your partner. When you share your reaction in a healthy way, you are building more intimacy.

ANGER VS. VIOLENCE

Some people stuff down their anger and don't express it at all. Some people swing to the other extreme—they uncork their anger in a big way! This can look like loud bouts of yelling, name-calling, and door slamming intermixed with cold silence, distance, and contemptuous looks.

Every once in a while, it's powerful to be able to express and be witnessed in your raw energy of anger. However, you may be thinking that anger is bad, wrong, and dangerous! Isn't the reason I'm reading this book so I can keep everything smooth?

You may be confusing anger with violence. Anger is healthy energy. Violence is not.

In the past, I, CrisMarie, have had these two intermixed and confused with each other—actually velcroed together. I grew up with an angry and violent father. And so, when Susan would get angry, I would cower. I needed to work on hearing and expressing anger in healthy ways. I needed to settle my nervous system and recognize I wasn't going to get hit if Susan shouted.

Anger is the energy of aliveness. In ancient Chinese medicine, it's the bursting forth of the life energy of wood growing. Anger is there to motivate you to take action on your own behalf.

Violence is very different. Violence is the crossing of someone's boundaries without their permission; for example, screaming in someone's face, grabbing someone by the arm, or breaking something.

It's helpful to look at and talk about what's in your personal filter around anger and violence. It's also natural in an intimate relationship to experience anger and to want to express your anger. If you don't, it can make things worse.

FRANK AND SALLY: ANGER

Take Frank and Sally, married thirty-two years with two kids. They stayed together for many decades, but had grown more and more distant—almost living separate lives. He had moved into another bedroom. They hadn't had sex in years. When he did come into her bedroom, she would ask him to leave.

When they came to work with us in Montana, as they approached different topics, they got nowhere. Each would wind up not feeling understood, and feeling hopeless, frustrated, and alone.

I, CrisMarie, was curious about the origins of their moving into separate bedrooms. What I heard was that he was too messy for her. Finally, with some prodding, Sally talked about him not treating her with respect. I got the impression this was not the whole story and asked her to say more.

When Sally opened up, she spoke of a Situation that had come up thirty years ago, after they'd had their first child. She'd wanted to have sex. She approached Frank to initiate sex, but he, in her words, recoiled from her. She had felt so much hurt and shame, assuming he was not attracted to her anymore. Eventually, she decided he no longer loved her.

Years and years went by. Sally kept believing this storyline ("He doesn't find me attractive" and "He doesn't love me") without ever checking it out with Frank to see if her beliefs were actually true. As the decades passed, her anger grew.

Truth be told, the same thing had happened for Frank, with anger piling upon anger.

We asked if Sally and Frank were willing to try something that we call Vesuvius[2].

---

2   Joann S. Peterson, *Anger, Boundaries and Safety*, (Gabriola Island, B.C. 2001), 70-73

TIP #5. TRY THE VESUVIUS EXERCISE...AND VENT YOUR ANGER!

A Vesuvius is exactly what it sounds like—a mighty, angry, erupting volcano. At times, it can be very healthy to allow yourself to "erupt" in this way—but with a few guidelines in place to protect your safety and that of your partner, too.

With this exercise, one person will be the erupting volcano for two minutes. The other person will be the silent observer and witness. Then you can switch roles. Here are the guidelines that we recommend:

1. No hurting yourself, other people, or property.

2. Decide together what the boundaries are—meaning, what's okay with both of you. This might include the area you can move in, swearing or not, and vocal volume. This is an opportunity for you to make this physical: you might want to stomp, shout, or pound the bed or couch. You can make this as physical as you want to within the agreed upon boundaries.

3. Take a few minutes before you start to do some deep breathing if you're having trouble accessing your energy.

4. Again, the time boundary is two minutes. At the end of the two minutes, you must stop immediately, even if you're right in the middle of a sentence.

5. If you want more time, you can negotiate an additional one or two minutes if your partner is open to it.

6. If the witness is worried about something, for example, that you may be getting too close to a dangerous object, they can call out, "Stop, [your name]"—and you agree to stop and check in before you resume.

As the witness, it can be tricky if all the anger is aimed at you. So, here are some tips:

- Breathe. Feel your Feet and Seat.

- Imagine an energetic boundary around you, remembering this is just energy venting, not truth or fact.

- You don't have to agree with anything s/he's saying—at all.

- At the end, it helps if you use your Reflective Listening skills. Take a moment to reflect back the gist of what your partner is expressing and their emotional tone, which is usually anger and hurt.

What if kids are present?

For those of you with kids, this can be empowering to do with them. Kids are masters at anger and tantrums. Plus, kids can feel when anger is there but being repressed. Some modifications you might want to consider:

- Maybe you don't use actual words, just let out the energy.

- You might want to say, "Blah, blah, blah" with the force of your energy.

- You can let the child be the time keeper.

When we encouraged Sally to do the Vesuvius, we coached her to breathe deeply for a few minutes before she started. Then we said "Go!" and started the timer. She let it rip.

"I am so angry with you! You think I'm ugly and disgusting. How dare you treat me so badly! I raised your two kids. I kept the house. I was loyal to you." Sally was stomping her feet and punching the air with her arms. "I supported you through medical school! Why didn't you love me?! Why did you reject me?! It's so unfair!… " It went on for a whole two minutes.

These were the words, yes, but Frank was also taking in Sally's energy. She was full of rage. Her cheeks were flushed. Her eyes were full of tears. It was clear she had gone through decades of telling herself that she was unlovable. When she finished, Frank looked stunned.

We asked Frank how he was. "Wow, I get how rejected you've felt. No wonder you're so angry and hurt." Then he asked if he could share more. She agreed. "I'm so sad you've felt this way for so long. I think you're beautiful. I recoiled because I knew you'd had an episiotomy. I didn't think you'd want me near you."

Wow! Sally was surprised by this information.

This was a major turning point for them. The opportunity to express the anger and be witnessed created a pathway for Sally to hear new information and for Frank to get the impact of his action of a very long time ago.

LET'S TALK ABOUT AGREEMENTS

As we have mentioned a few times, we believe it is crucial to hold back from trying to resolve a Situation too quickly. As you can see, it takes time to get to the heart of an issue.

Because you're a couple, even if you have a hot issue, you need to carry on with the business of living—parenting children and taking care of the home, your health, careers, finances, family, and friends. We suggest you make some agreements about how to keep your communication and relationship alive while in the midst of a tough (and potentially unresolved) Situation.

We find it's best not to have a long list of agreements, just a few that will keep you coming back to talk to each other and taking care of yourselves, especially when things get really tense. If you have too many agreements, they'll begin to feel like rules. Agreements are meant to be fluid and supportive. We suggest having one, two, or at most three agreements.

PROCESS FOR AGREEMENTS

Identify an area where you might need a new agreement.

- What is one Situation that feels really tough right now?
- What are key differences in what you each think is most important?

Discuss and/or write down what each of you wants in that Situation to feel good. (Try to use simple, straightforward language, for instance: "What I really want is _____ because _____."). Be sure to include your underlying core value.

Brainstorm ideas on what might work as an agreement.

Try out the new agreement and agree to adjust it as necessary.

We'll walk through an example.

Area: Having Tough Conversations

- Partner A: "When we have a disagreement, I really want to talk things through until we are complete."
- Partner B: "When we have a disagreement, I need time to myself to process what is going on."

You can see that each partner's needs and behavior negatively impact the other person.

Brainstorm What Each of You Want

- Partner A: "Even if you need time away to process, I want to know when you will come back to talk."

- Partner B: "If I come back based on a specified time period, I still may not want to talk."

Possible Agreement:

"When we are fighting and you (Partner B) need a time-out, we agree that we'll come back in an hour to check in and see if we can talk. If you (Partner B) are not able to talk then, you will let me know when we can talk. If it is more than a few hours, I (Partner A) can call our friend to get support."

CRISMARIE AND SUSAN'S AGREEMENT: REACHING OUT FOR SUPPORT

CrisMarie and I have an agreement in our relationship that if either of us decide that something is just too difficult to talk about, we'll call another couple for support. We didn't pick a therapist, we picked another couple. This is due to our extensive work with and trust in couples through our couples programs. We believe there's a higher likelihood that another couple will be able to support us in accessing our resources and finding our way through.

Don't get us wrong. We're not saying couples counseling or some therapeutic input might not be valuable. We just believe there is a lot to be said for finding other quality couples to support us working through our issues. Couples that come to our programs connect with others in this deep intimate way, making it easier to reach out when times are difficult.

TOM AND ALICE'S AGREEMENT: TRYING OUT A POLYAMOROUS RELATIONSHIP

Tom and Alice had been together for eight years and had a three-year-old. They'd both talked about the possibility of shifting to a polyamorous relationship for the last couple of years. Finally, Alice had given her okay, albeit with a bit of trepidation, to try it for a year. Within a week, Tom had made contact with a new woman and scheduled a first date. When they showed up to work with us, Alice was angry and upset. When we probed, it was clear that Tom had moved way too fast for her. She didn't believe him when he said he hadn't already had someone lined up when they made the agreement.

During the workshop, they had many heated discussions. Alice was frustrated that they hadn't talked about how, when, and who. She felt violated not knowing who Tom was essentially bringing into their relationship. Tom acknowledged he'd had his eye on someone but said he hadn't approached her until after he and Alice had made the decision. Then, it came time to talk about agreements. Alice wanted an agreement about their polyamorous endeavors.

Alice suggested, "Since we're a unit, when either one of us is having a polyamorous relationship, it's like bringing someone into our partnership. I want to request that we have regular communication about who we are going to be with and how it is for the other partner, and make sure the other partner feels comfortable with them." Tom blurted, "You've got to be kidding. You wouldn't feel comfortable with anyone I chose!"

Alice reminded him that she understood why this was so important to him and of her previously stated commitment to give this a go for a year. "I know you'll be with attractive women, successful women, younger women; women I will feel are a threat. I'm more worried about if I feel like someone is toxic or trying to get in between us."

Tom settled down and suggested, "So one agreement could be: If one of us believes a third party is toxic or is trying come in between us, we'll pause and discuss it?" Alice nodded, then added, "I want two agreements. We'll each be willing to process how it is for the other as we go—especially if one of us feels threatened, small, and/or jealous." Tom agreed.

BARB AND CAL: GETTING TO THEIR AGREEMENT

Barb and Cal joined us in Whitefish for one of our Couples Mojo programs. During the four days, the biggest transformation occurred when Barb acknowledged there were a number of things she was not saying and was fearful to even start to address. When we work with couples in Montana, we have some extra special guests at the event: horses.

WHAT IS EQUUS WORK?

Horses are remarkable for their ability to give clear, direct, and rapid biofeedback. This feedback enables people to deepen their awareness of themselves. As a result, working with horses can shine a spotlight on the key patterns that may be blocking people from creating the connections they want. Through a facilitated process, couples can translate the feedback coming from the horses. You are also in relationship with the horse. Interpersonal relationship dynamics are often played out with the horse, which makes them easier to see and understand.

Barb finally started to open up after some work out in the arena with a horse. She and Cal had been attempting to move a horse through some obstacles set up around the arena. Cal, the more experienced horse person, was being quite directive and putting Barb into situations she judged to be uncomfortable. Finally, she stopped the process and shared that this was too familiar. Their relationship was built around Cal controlling everything—from the finances to when they had sex, to when and where they would take vacations—and now, the horses!

Barb was almost in tears as she spoke. Cal started to respond; however, the horse stepped in first and walked gently to stand just behind Barb. This was the first time the horses had come this close. As Barb cried, the horse simply stood beside her. Cal was very moved by the experience with the horse, which provided an opportunity for Barb to finally speak her truth.

We invited Barb to keep sharing what she hadn't been saying. Cal walked beside her as she spoke. The horse maintained a position just behind her as she walked.

With the outdoor arena being so large, we don't know all that they shared, but Barb, Cal, and the horse walked for about twenty minutes together. Both Barb and Cal reported that this was one of their most honest and real conversations ever.

When it came to talking about agreements, Cal joked, saying, "Well, I guess we need to get a horse. It seems to be the only way I make enough space for Barb to speak…and the only way I can listen!"

What was so powerful about this revelation was that Cal didn't say "because Barb doesn't speak up." No. Instead, he owned his struggle to listen.

We knew that the real agreement wasn't going to be about finding a horse, but about finding a way to open space for Barb to speak up and for Cal to listen…not just in arenas and stables, but at home, too.

What they agreed to do was use the 5-5-5 tool on a regular basis when making decisions and plans—and that Barb would go first. They also agreed to come back again for another couples intensive in Montana using the horses, with the intention to brush up their communication skills in the future.

WHEN IS ENOUGH...ENOUGH?

We want to be clear that while we believe many differences between you and your honey can come to creative solutions, we also know there are times things don't work out. There are times when you each want two very different things.

So what if even after trying all the tools, you still can't come to an outcome that feels right for you both? How long do you try to hash it out before you decide this isn't going to work? How do you know when to call it quits, go your separate ways, and choose the ME over the WE?

You know it's time to call it quits when staying feels like you're dying a little inside. You'll know when you feel it. It means you're bending too much, sacrificing too much. Remember, we started this book with relationship math:

1 person x 1 person = 1 whole relationship

½ person x 1 person = ½ relationship

½ person x ½ person = ¼ relationship

When the relationship math deteriorates, when one of you has given up too much of your essential self—you and the relationship both suffer.

We find this happens in couples when they have diverging—or mutually exclusive—core values. For example:

- One of you wants kids—the other is adamant that they don't.

- One of you wants a polyamorous relationship—the other is devoted to monogamy.

- One of you wants to be a nomad traveling the globe—the other wants to build a stable home.

AMY AND BRADY

We were working with a couple, Amy and Brady, who'd been together for over five years and owned a home together. They had a great relationship, enjoyed each other, and had rich discussions and fun together. Then, Brady decided he wanted to become polyamorous. Like troopers, they picked up the tools we provided. Amy and Brady started having tough conversations, each trying to settle their nervous system while engaging in discussion, using the 5-5-5 and even the *Check It Out!* tool.

As they discussed their Situation, Brady was clear in his desire to have other intimate partners. Amy wondered, "Am I being closed-minded? Am I being a prude? Am I just being selfish?" She kept hanging in—trying to somehow make it work inside herself—but no matter how hard Amy tried to get comfortable with the idea of polyamory, it just didn't fit.

We suggested they go back to the boundary-ing process mentioned in Chapter 5: The ME. Amy realized she not only had a boundary, she had a bottom line. She wanted a committed monogamous relationship—sexual intimacy with only one person. Brady realized he too had a bottom line. He wanted intimacy with more than one person—polyamory.

So there they were with their mutually exclusive core values.

If either Amy or Brady chose to "settle," giving up what felt true for them, they'd be giving up too much of themselves, squishing themselves, or bending too much to make the relationship work—which ultimately wouldn't.

TRINA AND GREG

The same thing occurred with Trina and Greg, who had been together for three years. Trina wanted kids, while Greg, nineteen years her senior, already had kids and didn't want any more kids in his life.

A year after their initial conversation about kids, Trina was resigned to not having kids. She showed up in one of our online relationship programs, and she was trying to "get over it." When we reflected back how much she was sacrificing, she went home and had the boundary-ing conversation with Greg. There were many discussions, and in the end, she decided kids for her were nonnegotiable. A few months later, they split. Two years later, Trina is now pregnant and happy.

When you bump into your bottom line, your nonnegotiable—when it's just too important to you, it's time to prioritize ME over the WE.

BRINGING A RELATIONSHIP TO AN END

So, yes, there might come a time when you choose to end the relationship to preserve the wholeness of each person. You have choices about how to bring things to an end. It can be a horrendous, miserable process; or it can be as graceful and respectful as possible.

You can use these same tools in this book to come to a closure where you both feel whole.

Sure, it will be painful. You love this person. You may feel heartbroken. This is natural as you unravel your identity as this person's mate, your attachment to this person, and your sense of belonging. You may even second-guess yourself and think, "Well, it's been so good in the past, so why can't we figure this out?"

If you want to remain whole, to feel aligned inside your body, your heart, and your soul, make sure you're not bending too much. You can part ways with respect, and with a bit less turbulence and pain, even when you're struggling with a broken heart.

SUMMARY

Sometimes couples do decide that they will separate—but even in those situations, after deeper dialogue, the ending is very different. It can be amicable and respectful rather than crushingly painful.

It's so easy to fall into the trap of thinking your relationship is broken beyond repair. And yet, over and over, we have found that when there is time, space, and a willingness to be vulnerable and curious, couples discover they are NOT broken. They even come up with creative solutions they never thought of before.

We believe strongly that relationships—and particularly, intimate relationships—are the path to consciousness and transformation both for the individual, the couple, and the family.

Discovering ways to be loving and real even in your differences is powerful—and it is what allows you to relate through whatever Situation is presented.

BACK TO YOU

For your toughest issues, we suggest you invite your partner to do a 5-5-5 on the topic without needing to come to a solution right away. You may want to do a series of 5-5-5s. If you don't recall how to do the 5-5-5 exercise, reread the instructions on page 145.

See if you can identify, "Why is this so important to me?" What is the core value that is driving this for you? It may help you to break it down and use *Check It Out!* to get to the underlying core value for yourself. If you don't recall how to do the *Check It Out!* exercise, reread the instructions on page 134.

Also, ask your partner, "Why is this so important to you?" Really take the time to listen and reflect back what you're hearing. Remember that you don't need to agree. Just take in that this is how your beloved puts their world together.

Look at your own personal filter regarding anger and violence. What did you learn about anger and violence from your family of origin, from your parents, and from past relationships? How does that show up in your relationship today?

The next time you or your partner feel intensely angry, try out the Vesuvius exercise and see how you do. It may take practice to get it right. Keep trying.

What are one, two, or at maximum, three agreements that are important for you and your partner right now? Consider putting some brief agreements into place to help you both keep communicating.

Last but not least, we want to remind both of you to take your time. We can't emphasize this enough: don't try to rush to a solution. The tougher the Situation, the more time it may require to unpack everything and ultimately come up with a creative solution. Keep reminding yourself, "Yes, it is uncomfortable to be in this place of 'not knowing' and 'not having a solution.' However, this feeling of ambiguity won't last forever. We are moving in the right direction." Breathe deeply. Trust that you're moving in a beautiful direction…and that there's no need to rush.

CHAPTER 8

Before You Do That

Lastly, before you choose to have an affair (or make any other major decision about your relationship), read this.

We decided we couldn't wrap up this book without adding a few words about infidelity.

Thinking about having an affair? Please read this first.

It's not sexual attraction to another person that's a problem, it's how you handle that attraction that makes all the difference. Rather than have an affair, you have another choice.

Have you ever felt like your relationship is flat, dull, or even empty?

Then, you notice you're attracted to someone else. You begin to think, "Maybe I'm with the wrong person." You don't talk to your partner about any of this. Next thing you know, you're planning your day, your week, and your month around this other person. You start to dress differently; maybe you even start hitting the gym and getting in shape, or you cut your hair.

You feel so much more alive when you think about this other person. You relish when you bump into them, and even try to create opportunities for that to happen. You spend time daydreaming about what it'd be like if you did get together.

Until…your partner walks into the room.

Then, like a dieter trying to pretend you haven't been eating (or lusting after) chocolate, you shove thoughts of this other person out of your mind. You tell yourself, "No, it just can't happen. I'd better stop it." You hope your feelings will just go away.

That's your first mistake.

Hiding your feelings of attraction from yourself and from your partner is like trying to hold a beach ball underwater. It stays down only so long before it pops back up and smacks you in your face.

When you don't share what's really going on with your partner, it reduces the intimacy between you two, causing separation, which likely your partner can sense.

There you are, hoping your feelings for the other person will dissipate. Heck, maybe they do—until you see them again. Then the energy of the attraction rushes over you even more. This time, maybe you and your partner are having a fight, because your partner can tell you're hiding something. So you decide to open up about your marriage troubles to the other person.

That's your second and fatal mistake. You've just stepped onto a slippery slope.

Now, you've taken the emotional intimacy you had with your spouse and transferred it to this other person. Sound familiar? It's because you've seen this happen a hundred times before. Good movie scripts are made of this type of choice, but not healthy relationships.

You do have another option: reveal the attraction.

Yep, you heard us correctly. When you're daydreaming about the other person and your partner walks in the room, rather than trying to shove your feelings away, share them with your partner. Reveal there's someone who's caught your eye.

Okay, you may want to approach this delicately, but the main point is: Tell your partner. This increases the intimacy between you two, rather than between you and the object of your desire. You may start out with:

- "I've got something I want to share with you and I'm worried you may get upset."

- "I'm attracted to someone else. I want to share it with you, because if I don't tell you, I'm afraid I might act on it."

- "I'm attracted to someone else and I don't intend to act on it. Instead, I want to talk to you about the attraction."

- "I have something that's hard for me to say. I've got a crush on someone else. I don't intend to act on it. I think this crush is happening because I've been craving more [sex, passion, excitement, novelty, freedom, etc.] in my life lately. But I want to create those experiences with myself and with you—not with someone else. Can we talk about this?"

When you access your courage to discuss your attraction with your partner vulnerably, it discharges the energy of the "secret." You're revealing more about you—what fascinates you and excites you, which increases the intimacy in your primary relationship. You're showing up with your full ME by revealing more of you.

Sure, you may still find that other person attractive. We suggest you keep bringing your feelings back into your main relationship. It's not the sexual attraction, it's what you *do* with your sexual attraction that makes or breaks a relationship.

IF YOU'RE THE PARTNER WHO'S RECEIVING THIS "BREAKING NEWS," NO, IT ISN'T EASY

As the partner hearing about the attraction, it can be difficult to not make your spouse's excitement mean there's something wrong with you. It's natural to be thrown off. You may feel:

- Angry: "How dare you?!"

- Hurt: "After all we've been through?"

- Jealous: "You can't see her/him anymore!" or

- Insecure: "Am I just not pretty/young/rich/exciting/etc. enough for you?"

It may rattle your sense of attachment and trust in your partner and the relationship. It's easy to get caught in the trap of thinking "s/he isn't attracted to me anymore." This isn't necessarily true. Sexual attraction to other people is healthy and normal—yes, even when you're in a committed relationship. It means you're a living, breathing human being. So is your partner.

When your partner is talking about their attraction, see if you can access your curiosity. Think of it as if your partner is telling you about a piece of art they awakens their excitement, moves them, or inspires them. Wouldn't you want to hear what it is about that painting, music, or sculpture that grabs them so, and what goes on inside when they experience it? Don't you want to know what they're yearning for? Rather than thinking it's all about your deficits, consider that it's about their desires.

We're not saying this is easy, but it is important. If you don't want to hear about your spouse's attractions, you shut down the connection between you, which can be deadly. This happened with Ana and Steve.

ANA AND STEVE

Steve was attracted to Christine, a coworker. Rather than act on it, he told Ana about the attraction. In fact, he wanted Ana to meet Christine as a way of reducing the secrecy and charge. Unfortunately, Ana was too upset. She didn't want discuss Christine or meet Christine as a couple. This put Steve in the position of having to choose. They couldn't discuss it, which for Steve brought up other issues in the relationship. Eventually, it broke Ana and Steve apart.

Contrast that with Jane and Bob. Jane also had an attraction at work. She came home and told Bob that she was attracted to Dean, the new salesman. At first, Bob was jealous, but then he got curious about what was so interesting about Dean. Jane revealed how she found Dean sexy because he was so worldly and traveled, something Jane had always wanted to do with Bob. After talking about the importance of travel, they decided to take a weekend getaway. It wasn't long until they each started sharing who they found attractive and why. It revitalized their lovemaking. Now, whenever they go out on date night or when they take vacations, which they now regularly do, they play the game, "Who would you do and why...?"

If you're in a long-term relationship, it's inevitable that you're going to be attracted to other people at some point or another. Learning to discuss your attractions with each other will create more resiliency within the relationship rather than breaking it apart.

CLOSING THOUGHTS

You've arrived at the end of this book!

We hope you have enjoyed it and have been practicing a few of the tools that we've shared. We have a few thoughts we want to leave you with in parting.

We call this book *The Beauty of Conflict*—not *The Fun of Conflict*, not *The Ease of Conflict,* nor *The Feel-Good of Conflict.* We're not going to lie. This journey into emotional intimacy—into-me-see—is not always fun, easy, or full of glorious feelings. This is a journey that requires courage and a willingness to tolerate discomfort and uncertainty. However, it's a journey that is absolutely worth it. Because through this journey, you get to experience one of the greatest rewards that any human being can experience: a deeply loving, committed, and healthy relationship.

Our hope is that you'll use the concepts and tools that we've shared to create a deeper connection to yourself, to your true desires, and to your partner. We hope you'll access your courage and speak up with vulnerability. We hope you'll engage your curiosity as well as listen, really listen, to your partner's point of view. We hope you'll remember to breathe, slow down, and settle your nervous system when you're feeling emotionally charged up so that you can discuss hot topics more effectively. And through this work, we hope that amazing creative solutions will emerge—solutions that neither one of you were previously able to see clearly!

Victor Hugo once said, "To love another person is to see the face of God."

Your relationship with your partner is like an invisible container. Inside this container, both of you have the opportunity to grow and expand, to love and be loved, to live into your potential, and to "see the face of God."

To love and be loved in return—what a gift and privilege that is. Giving and receiving love is probably as close as we humans can come to experiencing "God," "divinity," or "heaven" while living right here on earth.

Go forth, knowing your relationship journey will inevitably have peaks and valleys. But if you're willing, each of you can stay together, grow together, and continue creating aliveness, passion, and intimacy with each passing year.

We're rooting for you.

CRISMARIE AND SUSAN

RESOURCES

When your relationship isn't thriving, it can feel so discouraging and isolating. Please remember that you are not alone on this journey. There are millions of people who understand the pain you're experiencing, and there are thousands of resources available to you. No matter where you live, and no matter what your circumstances or budget may be, you can get the support you need to help yourself and your relationship. You don't have to walk this path alone.

WORKING WITH US

We're here to support you. We offer a number of services, including coaching for couples, coaching for individuals, online programs, and workshops in Montana (where we live) and on Gabriola Island in British Columbia, Canada. You're welcome to attend a workshop with your partner—or by yourself. Either way, you'll leave with new tools to handle conflict differently and improve your relationship.

At our workshops, you'll have space to share everything that's going on in a calm, supportive, safe setting. You'll experience beautiful scenery, fresh air, time in nature, and (in Montana) an Equus coaching experience with therapy horses, which can create profound emotional breakthroughs.

Visit our website for details on our services: www.thriveinc.com

SUPPORT GROUPS

Perhaps you'd love to attend a relationship workshop—but money's very tight right now. If you're on a limited budget, consider joining a free support group in your city—or online. It's not the same as working with a trained professional, of course. However, joining a group can provide a feeling of relief and hope during a challenging time. It always feels good to know, "I'm not alone."

One website where you can search for events and gatherings in your local area, including love and marriage support groups, polyamory support groups, divorce support groups, and many others is meetup. com. Whatever type of situation you're experiencing, check meetup. com, because there's probably a group for you.

If you'd prefer to connect with people online, go to psychcentral. com and look for "forums and support groups." You can create a confidential profile, log in, post a message to share your story, and receive words of support and encouragement from people who understand what you're feeling.

OUR FAVORITE BOOKS

Here are some of our favorite books on love, relationships, communication, navigating difficult situations, and transformation.

Mating in Captivity: Unlocking Erotic Intelligence by Esther Perel.

The Power of Vulnerability: Teachings on Authenticity, Connection and Courage by Brené Brown.

Conscious Loving: The Journey to Co-Commitment by Gay Hendricks and Kathlyn Hendricks.

Joining: The Relationship Garden by Jock McKeen and Bennet Wong.

Passionate Marriage: Sex, Love, and Intimacy in Emotionally Committed Relationships by David Schnarch.

OUR FAVORITE PODCASTS AND TALKS

Where Should We Begin, a podcast hosted by Esther Perel.

Rethinking Infidelity, a TED Talk given by Esther Perel.

The Power of Vulnerability, a TED Talk given by Brené Brown.

The Beauty of Conflict. We almost forgot to mention our own podcast! This is a show about handling conflict at work and at home, featuring interviews with clients who openly and generously share their stories with you. Look for the podcast on iTunes or on our website: www. thriveinc.com

ACKNOWLEDGMENTS

Writing a book is no small feat!

Creating this book required lots of brainstorming sessions on our couch at home…many discussions while riding around in the car, waiting in airport terminals, and taking long walks together… phone calls with advisors…and support from our wonderful tribe of colleagues and friends.

In no particular order, here are some people who helped make this book a reality:

We'd like to thank all the couples we have worked with over these past ten years. You have each been willing to open and shift and see your partner and your issues in a whole new light.

Thank you to Bennet Wong and Jock McKeen, the founders of The Haven Institute in British Columbia, Canada. Your willingness to engage in your relationship experiment with openness—sharing what worked and what didn't—was a huge inspiration for us stepping into our relationship as business and life partners. We also want to thank Cathy and Ernie McNally, David Raithby, and Sandey McCartney for partnering with us to create the Couples Alive Series at The Haven.

Alexandra Franzen, your ability to help us "alexize" our writing—and keep us moving—was powerful and made this process fun and fast.

Joanna Price, thank you for designing the cover for this book, and for being patient through multiple rounds of revisions to get it "just right." You make everything look fresh and beautiful.

To our publishing team at the Tiny Press/Mango Publishing. Thank you for taking our Word document and shaping it into an actual, real, hold-in-your-hands book.

To the many people who encouraged us to write this book: We know you're busy people with full plates, so please know that your words of support (even just a quick email to say, "Keep going") did not go unnoticed.

To our friends, family and colleagues who have supported our work and relationship: a special thanks to those of you who've been willing to hold a space when we've been in midst of conflict. (You know who you are!)

We couldn't have done this without you.

ABOUT THE AUTHORS

CrisMarie Campbell and Susan Clarke are the co-founders of Thrive, Inc. They work with individuals, couples, teams, and companies. They specialize in shifting people from stuckness, tension, and frustration into "oh, wow, we never thought of that!" solutions.

They've spoken at TEDx events, and they've worked with employees at companies like Johnson & Johnson, Microsoft, AT&T, Nationwide, San Francisco Giants, and the Bill and Melinda Gates Foundation.

Together, they've created dozens of workshops, webinars, and programs focused on communication, collaboration, creative problem-solving, partnership, teamwork, and successful strategies for managing conflict and stress at home and in the workplace.

Susan has a Master's degree in Applied Behavioral Science and has worked as a family therapist, relationship and Equus coach, and business consultant for over 20 years.

CrisMarie has a Master's in Business Administration and several coaching certifications. One time, years ago, she earned a spot on the US women's rowing team and competed at the Olympics.

CrisMarie and Susan are business partners as well as relationship partners. They're married and live in Montana, close to spacious fields and horses (Susan's favorite) and several good restaurants with excellent wine selections (which CrisMarie loves).

Learn more about CrisMarie and Susan's work at: thriveinc.com

OTHER BOOKS BY CRISMARIE CAMPBELL AND SUSAN CLARKE

The Beauty of Conflict: Harnessing Your Team's Competitive Advantage

This is our very first book in The Beauty of Conflict series. In this book, we share guidance geared towards companies and teams, not romantic couples. But our message is the same—namely, that conflict can be a beautiful thing! When approached with curiosity, conflict in the workplace can illuminate systems that aren't working, open the doors to much-needed conversations, and lead to exciting solutions.

How to Have Tough Conversations at Work

The Secret to Setting Boundaries That Stick

10 Phrases to Say to Your Honey In a Tough Conversation

These are three short "mini books" that you can download—for free—on our website. Visit: thriveinc.com/free-resources to download these books and other freebies, too.

Mango Publishing, established in 2014, publishes an eclectic list of books by diverse authors—both new and established voices—on topics ranging from business, personal growth, women's empowerment, LGBTQ studies, health, and spirituality to history, popular culture, time management, decluttering, lifestyle, mental wellness, aging, and sustainable living. We were recently named 2019's #1 fastest growing independent publisher by *Publishers Weekly*. Our success is driven by our main goal, which is to publish high quality books that will entertain readers as well as make a positive difference in their lives.

Our readers are our most important resource; we value your input, suggestions, and ideas. We'd love to hear from you—after all, we are publishing books for you!

Please stay in touch with us and follow us at:

Facebook: Mango Publishing

Twitter: @MangoPublishing

Instagram: @MangoPublishing

LinkedIn: Mango Publishing

Pinterest: Mango Publishing

Sign up for our newsletter at www.mango.bz and receive a free book!

Join us on Mango's journey to reinvent publishing, one book at a time.